W9-BGC-191
Entrepreneur
MAGAZINE'S
startup
Start Your Own
COIN-OPERATED
LAUNDRY
Your Step-by-Step
Guide to Success
Mandy Erickson
EP
Entrepreneur
Press

Editorial Director: Jere L. Calmes
Managing Editor: Marla Markman
Cover Design: Beth Hansen-Winter
Production: Eliot House Productions
Composition: Ed Stevens

This publication is designed to provide accurate and authoritative information in regard to the subject matter covered. It is sold with the understanding that the publisher is not engaged in rendering legal, accounting, or other professional services. If legal advice or other expert assistance is required, the services of a competent professional person should be sought.

Library of Congress Cataloging-in-Publication Data

Erickson, Mandy.

Start your own coin-operated laundry/by Mandy Erickson.

p. cm. —(Entrepreneur magazine's start up) (Entrepreneur Magazines's business start-up series; #1162)

Includes index.

ISBN 1-891984-87-X

1. Laundry industry—Management. 2. Self-service laundries—Management. 3. New business enterprise—Management. I. Title: Coin-operated laundry. II. Entrepreneur (Santa Monica, Calif.) III. Title. IV. Series. V. Entrepreneur business start-up guide; no. 1162.

HD9999.L382 E75 2003
648'.1'0681—dc21

2002192760

Printed in Canada

09 08 07 06 05 04 03

10 9 8 7 6 5 4 3 2

Contents

Preface

When I was working on this book, several people told me that they had considered opening a self-service laundry. “It seems like such an easy business,” they said. “You just set out the machines and people drop money into them.”

If you open a laundry with that attitude, I chided them, you can be sure your business will fail.

Running a laundry is like owning a café—customers will spend a good chunk of their day in your store, and they want to feel comfortable. If you or your staff welcome them, answer their questions cheerfully, listen to their life stories, they'll come back. When you decorate the store, keep it clean and the machines in working order, customers will bring their clothes to your laundry rather than the dingy place around the corner.

In short, the more effort you put into your laundry business, the more you'll get out of it, financially and personally. And that's where this book comes in: It'll help you get the most from your venture.

Perhaps most important, you'll learn how to research a location to see whether your business will sink or swim. You'll need to know, for example, whether the people who live near the store are likely to use laundries, or if most of them have washers in their homes. You'll discover when it's best to buy an existing laundry and when it makes more sense to build a new one. And you'll learn how to determine the value of a laundry for sale.

When you've found a location, this book will help you find the right equipment. You'll learn what the correct ratio of washers to dryers is and how to configure the machines so your customers can clean their clothes quickly and easily. This book will also give you some pointers for decorating your store in a way that draws customers inside. It includes ideas for extra services, such as a snack bar, Internet access, or a play area for kids.

In addition, you'll discover the pros and cons of staffing a laundry. While attendants keep the store clean and help customers, their salaries add more costs, and supervising adds headaches. Should you decide to hire attendants, this book will give you pointers on finding employees and keeping them motivated.

This book will also help you attract new customers to your store through advertisements and promotions. You'll hear from seasoned laundry owners about the marketing tactics that worked for them—and you'll save money by avoiding those that didn't.

Finally, you'll learn how to keep track of your finances so you can squeeze as much profit as possible out of your business. You'll know how to price your machines so you're competitive but still earning a buck, and you'll find out whether your employees justify their cost. You'll also get some tips on tax deductions specific to laundries.

As comprehensive as this book is, it can't tell you everything you need to know to start up a self-service laundry. A lot depends on your finances, your city and state, the competition in your area, the clientele, and your equipment. So I've included an appendix full of resources—including consultants, suppliers, associations, magazines, and manuals—to help you find answers to your questions.

Starting up a laundry business is a big commitment, emotionally and financially. You want to weigh your decisions as carefully as possible, consider all the options and be aware of potential downfalls. This book will help you do that.

1

The New Laundromat

The coin-operated laundry industry is currently undergoing a revolution. No longer dingy, unsafe, boring places that customers must endure on a weekly basis, laundromats are becoming fun and attractive multiservice centers that customers enjoy visiting. "The industry is now getting a facelift," says Brian Wallace, director of the Coin Laundry

Photo Courtesy: Laundromania

Association, a national association for self-service laundry owners. "There's a trend toward coin laundries being more comfortable for the customer."

The newer laundries have snack bars, a place to drop off and pick up dry cleaning, and computers with Internet access. Some of them don't even use coins. Instead, customers use swipe cards that subtract the cost of the wash or dry, much like a phone card or debit card. Many laundry owners also employ attendants to keep an eye on the store and help customers use the equipment.

If you're thinking about getting into the self-service laundry business, the first thing you need to have is a clear picture of the industry—where it's been and where it's likely to go. In this chapter, we'll take a look back at the history of laundromats, and we'll discuss current industry trends, as well as the market outlook. In short, we'll give you the skinny on what you need to know before launching your own laundry business.

Laundromat Renaissance

The coin-operated laundry industry is changing in response to several trends currently impacting the business. The first is that, for most of us, meeting the demands of work and our personal lives leads to a time crunch—there just aren't enough hours in the day to accomplish everything we would like. Laundry owners are capitalizing on this reality by offering their customers timesaving convenience in the form of *wash-and-fold* (drop-off service) and dry-cleaning service. Some are even picking up laundry from customers' homes and delivering it back to them clean and folded.

Janet H., who runs a laundry in Fullerton, California, has had great success with her wash-and-fold service. "With the economy being so much better and so many women working, it occurred to me that drop-off service might work," says Janet. Her instincts were right on target, and she has profited by accommodating her customers with a service that saves them both time and energy.

Bright Idea

If you have a friend who's a manicurist, a palm reader, a masseur, or something else that could complement your business, ask if he or she wants to offer those services in your laundry. Your friend will benefit from the captive audience, and you may draw more business from people who want to get their nails done and their clothes washed at the same time.

In addition, owners have realized that they can maximize their profits by providing customers with access to multiple services. Since they're paying a set amount of rent on their commercial space, they might as well use that space to its fullest potential. Many owners around the country are serving food, renting mailboxes, and offering free Internet access. These additional services draw extra income for laundry owners, with little increase in overhead because the rent is already paid. Customers benefit by being able to use several services all in one convenient location.

"More operators are looking for additional ways to generate income," says Paul Partyka, editor of *American Coin-Op*, a magazine devoted to self-service laundries. "You're seeing operators try a variety of services: Some make keys, some do photo developing, and some do video rental. They're basically looking to utilize their space as profitably as possible. They are treating it more as an overall business than just a coin laundry."

Another trend laundry owners have recognized is that customers prefer to visit laundromats with a more pleasant atmosphere. Many laundry owners are building kids' centers, holding music concerts, giving away free coffee, and hiring attendants who are friendly and helpful.

Craig H. and his business partner, Tom L., have opened stores in three cities in Washington state. They have watched their profits grow, despite nearby competition. Craig attributes this to the fact that nearby laundries are smaller and offer fewer services. At his laundries there are wash-and-fold services, play areas for children, and attendants who are on duty at all times. "We thought there was an opportunity to bring it to a new level, with better machines, cleanliness standards, and customer service," Craig tells us. The tactic worked, and Craig's sales are climbing.

The Good News

Figures from the U.S. Census Bureau suggest that as the population of the United States grows, the number of renters—your main market—is likely to grow, too. Other social phenomena, such as the prevalence of two-income families, suggest that convenient services such as wash-and-fold will continue to grow in popularity as working parents have less time to attend to household chores like laundry.

According to Partyka, the wash-and-fold business saw a 15 percent growth last year. Partyka also notes that even people with washers and dryers at home are using self-service laundries for the sake of convenience. With the regular capacity machines used in homes, it can take quite a lot of time to do load after load—that's where laundromats come in. "They just run over to the coin laundry, use a couple of the large machines and knock it off," he says. In other words, although the majority of laundromat customers are low- to middle-income renters, some laundries are tapping into higher-income markets by offering convenience: wash-and-fold service and large machines.

In addition, office dress codes are growing increasingly less formal. And as more people wear casual clothing (which doesn't require dry cleaning) to work and leave the nicer duds for special occasions, you may find that consumers will be making more trips to the laundromat.

The Bad News

While the trends we've mentioned are favorable for entrepreneurs entering the laundry business, they don't suggest that business is booming. The industry is what

Give and Take

According to *American Coin-Op* magazine, these are some typical prices that laundry owners charge for using the following equipment or services:

Top-load washer:	$1.25 per load
18-pound front-load washer:	$1.75 per load
25-pound front-load washer:	$2.50 per load
35-pound front-load washer:	$3.00 per load
Dryer:	$0.25 per 10 minutes
Wash-and-fold:	$0.85 per pound
Vended detergent:	$0.50 per box

experts describe as a "mature market." Save for areas that are seeing high population growth, pretty much every neighborhood that needs a laundry has one—or two or three that are competing vigorously. In some areas of the country, there are too many laundromats already.

However, there is room for new laundry owners. Many get into the business by purchasing an existing laundry and renovating it. Some also find that they can build a new laundry in an area with competing laundries and thrive by offering a bigger store, more services, and better customer relations. Another way to get into the business is to locate your store where there is the best potential need for a new laundry: in an area that's experiencing population growth.

So as you consider getting into the laundry business, keep the words "mature market" in mind. Don't buy a store just because it's for sale or build a store just because you have a great idea for a new gimmick. You'll need to be very careful to make sure there's enough of a customer base to make your business thrive. You may be able to draw a little extra business from people who like using your store better because of its cleanliness or from people who use your wash-and-fold service, but the core of your business will be people who just want to get their laundry done quickly and conveniently. If there are already enough laundromats in the neighborhood to serve their needs, they're not as likely to patronize your store.

Finally, you also need to consider that getting into the laundry business requires a large initial investment. The average-size laundromat will cost you in the neighborhood of $200,000 to $500,000—whether you choose to purchase an existing laundry or build one in a retail space.

The Annals of Laundromats

Let's step back for a minute to see how the self-service laundry industry got to where it is today. It all started with the first wringer washer, built in 1907. During the Depression, enterprising businesspeople started using wringer washers to operate public laundries. These businesses were originally drop-off services, where customers left their laundry to have someone wash it for them.

Later on, customers could rent the machines to use themselves. "People took wringer washers and put them in a building," says Lionel Bogut, a laundry expert (owner, distributor, and consultant) who's been in the business for 50 years. "They would tap hot water to each of the washers, and people would come in and rent them for an hour or two."

Electric washers were not produced until the late 1930s. When manufacturers eventually added coin slots to the machines in the late 1950s, true coin-operated laundries came into existence. A coin-laundry construction boom followed. There was

Fun Fact

One of the earliest washing machines was designed so that you could hook it up to the engine of a Model T Ford. If you didn't have a Model T, you could still operate it by pumping with your hand or foot.

such a high demand for these stores that anyone who built one was almost guaranteed a profit. The owners of coin-operated laundries didn't need to keep their stores clean and machines working to attract customers and make a profit. As a result, many laundromats were kept in poor condition.

The industry deteriorated as broken machines stayed broken, stores were left dirty, and vandals and thieves took advantage of the lack of owners' attention. In the 1960s, however, the industry experienced a resurgence. Smart new investors realized they could do better than run-down, unattended stores and started creating spiffy new businesses. They built larger stores, hired attendants, and added dry cleaning and clothing repair.

This revitalization didn't last long, though. During the oil crisis of the 1970s, the industry saw another downturn as energy costs cut into profits and rising interest rates scared off new investors. But the industry recovered in the 1980s, due in large part to the production of new, energy-efficient equipment by manufacturers. Since that time, the number of laundromats has steadily grown; today there are approximately 30,000 to 35,000 laundromats countrywide.

Move Over, Guys

While the laundry business has traditionally been male dominated, more and more women are running their own laundromats and working as experts in the industry. Two trade magazines—*New Era Magazine* and *The Journal*—boast female editors, and regional coin laundry associations typically have a healthy share of female members.

The fit is natural, says Janet H., a laundry owner in Fullerton, California, and one of the pioneers in the business. Having owned and run laundromats for 26 years, Janet says the laundry business is a good one for women. Many women already "know laundry" from the experience they accumulate while taking care of this task for themselves and their families. In addition, a laundry business can be run part time, so women can often take care of young children and still have time to manage the business.

The Laundromat Life

If you're planning on operating just one or two stores, you'll be in good company. The industry is composed mostly of small-business owners who operate one or maybe two stores. While there are no national laundry chains, a few local chains are starting to grow in various parts of the country. These chains are still quite localized, though, and few consist of more than a handful of stores.

"For most people, a coin-op is a moonlighting," says Wallace of the Coin Laundry Association. "They have other businesses, or they have a day job." However, he adds, "It's not a very homogeneous business." More laundry owners are starting to own larger stores and more than one store. These people are able to survive on the income larger stores or multiple stores generate.

The amount of money you can make from a laundry varies tremendously. According to Wallace, the annual gross income from one store can range from $30,000 to $1 million. The expenses incurred while running a store range between 65 and 115 percent of the gross income. That means that for a store grossing $30,000 per year, at best it earns $10,500, and at worst it loses $4,500. For a store grossing $1 million per year, the profit could be as high as $350,000, or there could be a loss of up to $150,000, depending on expenses.

Wallace says these profit margins have less to do with the size of the store than with its owner. An owner who runs his or her store well—who keeps it clean, repairs its equipment quickly, uses energy-efficient systems, and offers good customer service—will see profit margins of 25 to 35 percent.

The steady income that a laundry generates is a plus for many people. If you're looking for a business that will keep the cash flowing no matter what the rest of the economy is doing, you've found it in laundries. Clean clothes are a necessity, not a luxury, so people are going to use laundromats no matter how the stock market is performing. The business is also fairly steady month in, month out. So unless you draw on vacationers' dollars in a place with seasonal tourism, you'll find that you can count on a fairly steady income throughout the year.

But remember, the laundry business is not growing; it's mature. There are about as many stores as there is dirty laundry to fill them. To ensure your business will survive, you'll need to make sure your laundromat is in a location that's convenient for people who use laundromats. And to make your business thrive, you'll need to give your customers

Stat Fact

According to *American Coin-Op* magazine, the top expenses for laundry owners include rent, utilities, employees, loan payments, taxes, maintenance and parts, and insurance.

something they don't get in other laundromats—a nice atmosphere, good customer service, and entertainment.

By now, you should have a much clearer picture of what the industry looks like. The next thing you'll need to think about is whether the laundry business is the right fit for you. In Chapter 2, we'll delve into what it's really like to own a laundry store, and we'll give you an idea of the personality traits that are best suited to this kind of business.

2

Is It for You?

Now that you know the history of the laundry business and where it's headed, you'll need to think about whether running a laundromat is the right business opportunity for you. Does it suit your personality? Do you know what a typical "day in the life" is like? This chapter is designed to help you tackle these questions and see if the laundry business is a good fit.

No Experience Necessary

None of the entrepreneurs interviewed for this book had experience in the laundry business when they first started. One had a resume that included milking cows, another was a contractor, and yet another was a retail manager. Most just decided that starting a laundry was a good business opportunity. However, they all recommend that new entrepreneurs research the business by talking to laundry owners, joining associations, and reading the trade literature.

"My partner and I looked at dozens of laundries in the local area, and we did some traveling," says Craig H., the laundry owner in Washington state. "We asked if we could hang in the laundries and work there, which we did." The two of them also attended a Coin Laundry Association convention in Chicago and took a tour of laundries in the area.

Collette C. knew nothing about the business before she started a laundromat in Evans, Colorado, with Kim C., her business partner. But the two got to work when Collette's uncle, who was building a strip mall, asked if she'd be interested in operating a laundromat. "We did a lot of research," Collette says. They spoke to a number of laundry owners about the business and read as many issues of trade magazines as they could find.

"Be patient and do your homework," advises Brian Wallace of the Coin Laundry Association. "You'd be absolutely amazed how quickly someone will get into business and spend their life savings without doing any research whatsoever."

While no particular experience is necessary, a business background is always important. In addition, a background in machine repair or a knack for fixing machines helps. Owners who have experience with laundry equipment are able to cut down on the cost of repairs. But others have found that they can learn about the machines and make some repairs themselves, or hire a repairperson and avoid the headache altogether. The self-service laundry business is an open club. With enough enthusiasm, interest, and business-savvy, you can join the club and succeed in the industry.

The Laundromat Personality

You may think that the laundry business is about clothes, but what it's really about is people. It's a service business, and like any service business, you need to treat your customers well if you want them to return to your store.

If you're friendly, your customers will want to use your store. By taking the time to talk to them, you will also be able to learn about their laundry needs and their preferences for services. Ultimately, this kind of information will help you improve the quality of your business so that you can attract even more customers.

Even if you decide to hire employees and leave the customer relations to them, you still need good people skills to hire and supervise employees. The more closely you work with them, and the better they know and like you, the better job they'll do.

If you have an unattended laundry that you visit twice a day to clean and collect quarters, you still need to greet your customers with a smile on your face and an attitude that's ready to help. So if small talk with strangers leaves you cold, and you can't stand the thought of answering customers' questions (often the same ones over and over), the laundry business may not be the one for you.

Bright Idea

When you talk with other laundry owners to learn about their experiences with the business, avoid your own neighborhood. Your competitors will be reluctant to help you out, and you don't want someone giving bad advice in the hope that your business will fail.

However, if you think you'll like meeting new people, helping them work the machines, and listening to them talk while they wait for the dryers to finish, you'll find this business rewarding. "I've enjoyed it; I've really enjoyed it," says Janet H., the laundry owner in Fullerton, California. "It's been very good for me. I love people. When I go to my store, it lifts me off the ground."

Suit Your Style

The good news about owning a laundry is that you can shape your business to fit your own tastes. You can hire employees, offer a variety of *fabricare* services, and run a full-fledged operation; or you can keep things simple by opening a small, unattended laundry. The other piece of good news is that you don't need a background in running laundromats or taking care of laundry equipment, though you do need to research the business.

The bad news is that you need lots of money upfront to buy an existing laundry or to build one in a leased space ($200,000 to $500,000 on average). And while you can earn money from a laundry while you work elsewhere, you still need to keep the store in good working order by supervising employees, fixing machines, and collecting the money.

Self-Help

The beauty of owning a self-service laundry is that your customers help themselves. You don't have to be at your store; you don't even have to hire someone to be at your

> **Bright Idea**
> If you're not sure you'll like the laundry business, try working in a laundromat for a while. Volunteer at a nearby store or take a temporary job. You'll have a much better idea of whether the business is for you after working in a laundry, even after only a few days.

store. You can work at another job or run another business while your customers are dropping coin after coin into your machines. For entrepreneurs who don't want the hassle of hiring employees and writing paychecks, this is a big incentive.

"I like the fact that it's pretty stress-free," says Brian D., who owns an unattended laundry in Iowa City, Iowa. "The laundry business is really a breath of fresh air." Brian's other job is running an equipment rental business, so he's always worried about having enough employees and equipment to respond to customers' demands. The laundromat, on the other hand, requires only a quick visit twice a day to clean and collect money. He rarely has an emergency, except when a machine breaks and he needs to call a repairperson or make an extra visit to fix it.

Janet H., who has owned several different laundromats over 26 years, agrees that laundries can be low-maintenance. Her first stores, which she bought during the 1970s, were unattended. She hired someone to clean the laundries and someone else to maintain equipment, so the only time she visited was to collect money. This was

Top Seven Headaches

Every year *American Coin-Op* magazine conducts a survey of its readers to find out what the top problems are for laundromat owners. The list varies little, says Paul Partyka, editor of the magazine. "The order may change, but the issues are the same every year," he says. So if you're like most other laundromat owners, you can expect to face the following challenges in running your business:

- A shortage of good employees
- The high cost of utilities
- Charges for water and sewer lines
- Market saturation—too many laundromats in some regions
- Taxes
- Vandalism
- Abusive customers

important to her at the time because she had two young children and wanted to be home to raise them.

While the laundry business can be fairly stress-free, it can also interest entrepreneurs who want to take a more active role. Owners who hire attendants and offer wash-and-fold service have much more work to do, but they also reap greater financial—and personal—rewards. Now that her children are grown, Janet H. runs an attended laundry with wash-and-fold service. She visits the store every day to check on her employees and chat with customers.

Collette C. agrees that interacting with customers is the best part of the job. "I love the customers," she says. She enjoys talking with them and has come to know some of the regulars well.

Caring for Your Store

The laundry business might appeal to you because you don't have to work at it eight hours a day like other jobs. It's true—you can set out your machines and let them collect money while you do something else. But don't get carried away with the idea. Even if you don't have attendants to supervise, you need to make sure your store is sparkling clean, that equipment is working properly, that the change machines are full, and that your books are in order.

Tip...

Smart Tip

According to the Coin Laundry Association, the number-one rule for a successful laundry is to make sure it is always sparkling clean. People come to your store to clean their clothes, not dirty them. Never neglect to wipe down the washers and mop the floor.

"It isn't all about walking in and collecting your quarters and leaving," says Janet H. This was her approach with her first laundromats. Now that she's paying more attention to her store, she's finding the business much more lucrative and enjoyable.

And if you do hire attendants, they must be supervised closely. Most attendants make minimum wage or slightly more, so you can't expect them to take too active an interest in the success of your business. You must visit the store enough to be sure that it's running properly and employees are productive. For more information on motivating employees, see Chapter 9.

"Some people think 'Well, this is an easy business; I'll just hire someone and go play golf every day,'" says Paul Donovan, vice president of marketing and sales with PWS, a distributor of laundry equipment. "It doesn't work that way."

The Down Payment

You may not need a lot of free time or experience to run a laundry, but you do need a pile of cash. Whether you buy an existing laundry business or build a new one, you can expect to pay between $50,000 and $1 million. A typical laundromat, if such a thing exists, would be a 2,000-square-foot, relatively modest store in a shopping center. For one of these, you are looking at paying between $200,000 and $500,000.

"It is a capital-intensive business," says Wallace of the Coin Laundry Association. If you build a laundry, half of the start-up costs are the price of equipment, he says, and half are remodeling the space and installing equipment. But take heart: Some laundry owners have received loans from banks. In addition, equipment manufacturers and distributors will finance the cost of equipment.

The Daily Routine

So what's it really like to own a laundry business? Whether you do all the work yourself, or hire an attendant or a janitor, there are tasks you will need to take care of on a daily basis. You will need to open and close your store promptly each day, clean it, collect money, and fill vending and change machines. You will also need to keep track of which machines are being used and how often.

Those laundry owners who have attended stores will have other duties, too. They'll be hiring and supervising employees and overseeing additional services such as wash-and-fold. See Chapter 9 for information on providing extra services and overseeing employees.

The Hours You Shall Keep

Laundries are generally open between about 6 A.M. and 10 P.M. seven days per week. Because weekends are usually the busiest days for laundries, you should definitely keep your doors open on Saturdays and Sundays. In some instances, you may want to adopt alternate hours, especially if the market you serve or the location of your store lends itself to having open doors at other times of the day.

Brian D., who owns the laundry in Iowa City, keeps his store open 24 hours a day. His laundromat is in a college town, and students are notorious for keeping odd hours. "You've got the machines; you've already paid the money for the machines and the rent and everything else," he reasons. Because his laundry is unattended, he doesn't have to pay employees to stay up all night with his store.

> Tip...
>
> **Smart Tip**
>
> When cleaning your store, check the insides of the machines to make sure something left in a pocket didn't spill out and create a mess.

Other laundry owners we interviewed base their hours on surrounding businesses. Janet H., who runs a laundromat in a strip mall in Fullerton, California, locks up her laundry at

10 P.M. because that's when the Target store that anchors the mall closes. "The shopping center becomes desolate after that," she says, adding that she worries about the safety of her employees.

Dave A., who owns an unattended laundry with his wife, Kris, in New Glarus, Wisconsin, keeps their store open daily from 5:30 A.M. to 10:30 P.M. They chose those hours because they're the same hours the nearby gas station is open. "We feel it's working out perfectly," he says. "If we had kept it open later, we might have had more vandalism."

> **Dollar Stretcher**
>
> You can buy a stainless steel cleaner from your distributor to wipe down those stainless steel machines, or you can use a simple solution of ammonia and water. Wash with some clean rags, and wipe the machines down when you're done. If you want to polish them, just use baby oil.

Your first duty of the day is to open your store, and you must be on time because your customers may plan their day around getting their laundry done at a certain time. You can avoid having to be at your store early in the morning and late at night by installing an automatic lock system on a timer. A typical system like this will cost you between $3,000 and $5,000.

New Glarus laundry owners Dave and Kris A. installed an automatic system in their store. "It opens itself and locks itself," Dave says. The lights are also on a timer. Since both Dave and Kris have other jobs, the system has been invaluable to them.

At night, of course, you must close down and lock up. If you want all the customers to be gone by 10 P.M., you should consider locking the door at 8:30 P.M., leaving enough time for the last loads of laundry to be finished. You can either let customers out yourself, or install a lock system that allows them to leave but prevents others from coming inside.

Scrub-A-Dub-Dub

Why do people visit a laundromat? They want clean clothes. As obvious as this may be, the operative word here is *clean*. No one wants to fold their clothes in a pile of dust and cigarette ashes, or place their clothes in a dryer coated with lipstick (it happens). "Just make your place look nice and bright and clean," says Brian D.

The first order of business for you or an employee you hire is to clean your store thoroughly at least once a day. This will take about two to three hours. You or your employee will need to do the following:

- Mop the floors
- Wipe down the machines
- Clean the soap dispensers in your front-load washers
- Wash off the folding tables

- Clean the bathroom
- Empty the trash
- Wash the windows
- Clean the vending machines, change machines, and video game screens

The best time to clean is after customers have gone—that way you or your employees can clean more efficiently. You'll also avoid the risk of customers slipping on wet floors or tripping over cleaning equipment. If you have a large or busy store, however, you may find that it requires cleaning twice a day. You can wipe down the machines and folding tables easily while customers are in the store, but save the floor for after they've left or for a slow period of the day.

Collecting Coins

One chore you're not likely to delegate to an employee is collecting money from the machines. If you have a card system (see Chapter 7 for more on card systems),

The Land of Lost Coins

You may hear customers complain that they put money into a machine, and the machine didn't work. Naturally, you want to keep your customers happy, so you need to refund their money as quickly as possible. One way to do this is to post your phone number in the store and have customers call if they lose money. Alternatively, you can have them drop notes in a box.

Brian D., who owns an unattended laundromat in Iowa City, Iowa, has set up a drop box in his store along with a stack of tickets and instructions on what to do if a customer loses money. The tickets have two parts. On one part of the ticket, the customer writes his name and address, and the amount of money he lost. This part of the ticket goes in the drop box. The other part, which reads, "Broken," gets placed on the offending machine.

How do you know customers are telling the truth? That's a risk you might want to take. The refund won't cost you much, and if the same customer asks for more than a few refunds, then you can be suspicious. Brian says that he's usually able to verify when someone has lost money. For example, if a customer claims she lost $5 in the change machine, he knows she's telling the truth because he'll find a jammed fiver in the machine when he opens it up. He adds that he hasn't found that anyone has tried to take advantage. "A lot of times I think people are just interested in getting the problem fixed," he says.

> **Tip...**
> ### Smart Tip
> You may find that the soap dispensers in your front-load washers are caking with soap scum that's nearly as hard as stone. The scum is from soda ash, used as filler in inexpensive detergents. Try using a brush with hard bristles to remove the deposits. If that doesn't work, you can purchase a commercial descaler.

your job is much easier. All you'll have to do is empty the card machine of the bills, count them and deposit them in the bank.

But if you have a coin laundry, you'll need to empty each machine, preferably daily. You'll want to pull (take out the coins) from one type of machine at a time so you can determine how much your customers are using each type of machine. Put a bag in one of your laundry baskets and roll it from machine to machine, starting with the top-loaders. Count these coins and record how much money you made on this type of machine, then follow the same procedure with the front-loaders and the dryers.

For recording purposes, you should use a chart similar to the "Equipment Use Chart" we've provided on page 19. Draw up a chart with seven rows, one for each day of the week, and columns for each type and size of equipment: top-loaders, front-loaders, dryers and vending machines. Then record in your chart how much money you withdraw every day. We'll discuss what to do with the information later in this chapter.

You should refill the change machine in your store on a daily basis, too. When it's empty, your customers can't do their laundry, and they'll go elsewhere. If it's empty more than a few times, they may never return. No one wants to lug several loads of laundry to a laundromat, only to find they can't get change. Brian D. says if his change machine runs out, "That's like shooting myself in the foot. I check the change machine at least once a day."

> ### Bright Idea
> If you don't have a coin counter, but you want to know how much a bag of quarters is worth, weigh them. One pound of quarters equals approximately $20.

Safety Comes First

It's usually best to empty machines on a daily basis. You can do this once or twice a week instead, but you risk losing more money in case of theft or robbery. When you pull once a day, the most you'll lose is one day's take. When you pull coins (or bills in the case of card machines and change machines), there are a number of preventive measures you should take to ensure your safety.

- *Never try to pull coins or bills when no one's in the store.* You're handling lots of cash, and you don't want to leave yourself vulnerable.

- *Try to vary the time that you collect money so no one can plan a robbery.* In 26 years of owning laundries, Janet H., the Fullerton laundry owner, has never been robbed. Janet, who has owned eight stores, attributes her safety to varying the time she pulled coins each day. "I never went to the same store at the same time," she says.
- *Don't use a bank bag to collect money from your store.* A bank bag says to potential thieves, "I'm full of money; steal me." Put the money in a lunch cooler, briefcase, or purse—anything that doesn't look conspicuous.
- *Deposit the money in the bank as quickly as possible.* While this should be common sense, it's worth mentioning. Once you've taken care to collect the money from your machines safely, you don't want to put yourself at additional risk of robbery by carrying it with you any longer than necessary.

Let Us Vend

The last bit of daily business in your store is restocking the vending machines. If you own your own soda and snack machines, you will need to make sure they're full every day. If you contract with a vending company, they'll worry about filling them.

The most important vending machine in your store will likely be the soap vending machine, and since these machines are relatively inexpensive and rarely break, you should buy your own. Make sure it is properly stocked every day. Many customers will bring their own soap, but those who don't will expect to find soap available. An empty soap machine is almost as bad as an empty change machine—it will cause you to lose business.

Keeping Track

When you're done with the daily in-store duties, you'll need to take care of some additional office work. Many laundry owners do this at home, though some may find it easier to work in a rented office or at the laundromat if they have space. Craig H., the laundry owner in Washington state, rents a small office to take care of the paperwork. "We're pretty lean and mean, but I do have a small office away from the laundries," he says.

At your office, you'll need to take care of your accounting (we'll cover this in detail in Chapter 11), and you'll need to track equipment usage by customers in your store. It's important to record how often each type of machine is used so that you can determine if you've got the right mix of equipment. For example, if you find that your top-loaders are getting six turns a day (the number of times a machine is used each day) and your front-loaders only two, you may need to add top-loaders and remove some front-loaders. Your customers are likely waiting for the top-loaders and possibly going elsewhere, so you could be losing money.

It's probably easiest to track machine use weekly, using the record of money you collect on a daily basis. If you collect weekly, you can record the money you make each week. As you accumulate these records, you should convert them to monthly figures so that you can calculate your net income—by subtracting your monthly expenses from your gross monthly income. As with any business, you need to keep close tabs on income and expenses. With a laundry, you need to keep track of how much money

Equipment Use Chart

Use this chart to record how much money you've collected from each type of machine in your store. This will help you to keep track of which machines are getting the most use so you can find the best equipment mix for your store.

For the week of: ______________________

	Top-loaders	20-pound front-loaders	35-pound front-loaders	50-pound front-loaders	Dryers	Soap vending machine
Sunday						
Monday						
Tuesday						
Wednesday						
Thursday						
Friday						
Saturday						

each machine takes in and what each machine costs you (more on this in Chapter 11). Over time, you will be able to determine what equipment mix is best for your customers and your bottom line.

Next up: In Chapter 3, we'll take you through the ins and outs of market research. We'll also discuss how to put together a mission statement for your business.

3

Locating Your Market

One of the most important steps in starting a successful business is to make sure you do a thorough job of researching the market. Don't skimp when it comes to researching the laundry industry. You'll be investing hundreds of thousands of dollars in purchasing or starting a new laundromat, so you want to make sure it's a good investment. You need to know who your customers are, where they are, and what kind of competition you will face. The answers to these questions will be important in framing your business' purpose or mission statement. In this chapter, we'll focus on how to research the market and choose a good location for your laundry business.

Location, Location, Location

We've all heard the mantra "Location, location, location" when it comes to real estate. This mantra is vastly more important when you're purchasing a laundromat, or starting a new one, than when you're looking for a home. Don't let this mantra slip out of your mind for one second while you are researching locations. In fact, you should make sure to repeat it several times a day. A good location is extremely important for a laundry.

Laundry users head to the most convenient laundry. Customers aren't going to drag 30 pounds of laundry an extra half mile because they like the channel your TV is set to. They're also not likely to drive 30 minutes out of their way because they like the look of your machines. After all, the product—clean clothes—is the same no matter where they take their filled hampers. The California Coin Laundry Association estimates that 80 percent of your customers will use your laundry because of its location. Simply put: You need to be where your customers are.

Who Goes There?

When you're considering purchasing a laundromat, or you're thinking of leasing a site and building a new one, the first thing to do is take a good look at the surrounding neighborhood. Your customers will be people who don't have washers and dryers in their homes already. For the most part, this means apartment-dwellers. But it also means people who rent houses and lower-income folks who can't afford machines. So your best bet is to buy or open a laundromat in a low- to middle-income area surrounded by apartment buildings. "Usually with a laundromat you want at least 40 percent in that area to be renters," says Paul Donovan with distributor PWS. "That's where you are going to make your money."

Some homeowners with washers and dryers already in their homes will use your laundry on occasion for large items. However, they won't use it frequently enough to justify placing a laundromat in a well-heeled neighborhood full of single-family houses. And while these people may use wash-and-fold service, their business won't justify spending money on machines and paying the rent to keep them in the store. "You can't make it on comforters and sleeping bags," says laundry owner Janet H., who operates a store in Fullerton, California.

Bright Idea

If you're thinking of opening or purchasing a laundry in an area that attracts tourists, remember that vacationers need clean clothes, too. An ideal location would be one that's accessible to both the year-round crowd and the tourists.

Besides looking at areas full of renters, you'll want to purchase or develop a laundromat in an area that has many families with children. Not only are there more clothes to wash in larger families, but children tend to soil clothing more quickly (theirs as well as their parents'). Other regular laundromat customers include students and seniors, who tend to live in smaller quarters and often don't have laundry equipment in their homes.

Finally, look at how the neighborhood is changing. Are large, older homes being converted into apartments? That's a good sign. Or are developers kicking out the renters, razing the buildings, and replacing them with luxury lofts? That's a bad sign.

The Hard Facts

Once you've scouted out the neighborhood of your future laundromat, you'll need to go in search of some hard demographics. Your intuition may tell you the location is right, but when you're investing several hundred thousand dollars in one store, you'll want as much information as you can get. Demographics will give you the ages and income levels of the residents in the area, whether they rent or own property, how many children they have, and how the neighborhood is changing.

You can order census information from the government, from a demographic service or from the Coin Laundry Association (see the Appendix for contact information). Laundry equipment distributors can also supply you with demographic information. Check out pages 24 and 25 for a sample of the demographic information you might gather for a particular area.

Smart Tip

Tip...

You can get general demographics from the U.S. Census Bureau. Check out their Web site at www.census.gov. Click on State & County Quick Facts; choose your state and then your county. You can get general information about income levels and population growth for your county.

So let's review: A "good" neighborhood for a laundry has lots of renters with large families living on lower incomes, or one with lots of young, single people who rent. But also look at how the statistics for the neighborhood have changed over the years. If the number of renters has dropped, and incomes are rising, that's likely to continue and may not bode well for your laundromat. However, if the opposite is true, you may be looking at a growing customer base.

As stated above, most customers are going to visit the laundromat that's most convenient

Demographic Report

The chart below contains typical demographic information, with population figures, the number of owners vs. renters, and average household incomes listed for specific distances from the sample address (11974 Foothill). Demographics for areas within 0 to 0.5 mile, 0 to 1 mile, and 0 to 1.5 miles from the laundry address are listed. *(See sample location map on page 25.)*

PCensus for MapInfo

Profile Report
National Decision Systems 1998

Population Facts 1	11974 Foothill 0.00 - 0.50 mi		11974 Foothill 0.00 - 1.00 mi		11974 Foothill 0.00 - 1.50 mi	
Population						
2003 Projection	11,923		26,121		46,567	
1998 Estimate	11,139		24,368		43,658	
1990 Census	9,991		21,793		39,578	
1980 Census	6,397		13,555		27,000	
Population growth, 1980 to 1990	56.18%		60.77%		46.59%	
Households						
2003 Projection	2,644		6,331		10,535	
1998 Estimate	2,471		5,895		9,848	
1990 Census	2,250		5,357		8,969	
1980 Census	1,544		3,615		6,662	
Population growth 1980 - 1990	45.73%		48.19%		34.63%	
1998 Estimated population	11,139	% base	24,368	% base	43,658	% base
White	3,109	28%	5,940	24%	9,397	22%
Black	2,411	22%	6,042	25%	9,149	21%
Asian or Pacific Islander	788	7%	1,233	5%	1,580	4%
Other races	4,831	43%	11,153	46%	23,532	54%
Hispanic origin	7,840	70%	16,590	68%	32,501	74%
Occupied units	2,250	% base	5,357	% base	8,969	% base
Owner occupied	1,553	69%	3,501	65%	5,630	63%
Renter occupied	697	31%	1,856	35%	3,339	37%
1990 Average persons per household	4.21		3.91		4.26	
1998 Households by estimated income	2,471	% base	5,895	% base	9,848	% base
$150,000 or More	27	1%	74	1%	138	1%
$100,000 to $149,999	156	6%	340	6%	528	5%
$ 75,000 to $ 99,999	338	14%	597	10%	893	9%
$ 50,000 to $ 74,999	627	25%	1,497	25%	2,180	22%
$ 35,000 to $ 49,999	366	15%	812	14%	1,463	15%
$ 25,000 to $ 34,999	247	10%	812	14%	1,308	13%
$ 15,000 to $ 24,999	266	11%	749	13%	1,469	15%
$ 5,000 to $ 15,000	274	11%	751	13%	1,452	15%
Under $ 5,000	170	7%	263	4%	417	4%
Average household income	$ 52,424		$ 49,048		$ 45,771	
Median household income	$ 45,627 (Averaged)		$ 42,378 (Averaged)		$ 39,758 (Averaged)	
Estimated per capita income	$ 11,549		$ 12,098		$ 10,732	

Provided courtesy of PWS Inc.

Location Map

This map shows the location of the laundry at the sample address (11974 Foothill). The concentric circles indicate distances out from the address—0.5 mile, 1 mile, 1.5 miles. Demographic figures are provided for these areas in the report on page 24.

Provided courtesy of PWS Inc.

to them. If you're thinking of an urban location where customers are going to carry their laundry to your store, you can expect them to walk no more than half a mile. So if you're looking at an urban location, get demographic information within a half mile of the location you're considering.

If you are looking at a suburban location—usually in a strip mall with parking—you can expect customers to drive no more than five miles to your store. A rural location, however, will draw customers from as far as ten miles away. So if you will locate your laundry in either a suburban or rural locale, you should look at the demographics within five miles and ten miles of the site, respectively.

If you are considering purchasing or opening a laundry in an area that is growing, visit the city, township, or county the site is located in and ask for the General Plan. The plan will show what areas are slated for businesses, what areas are designated for low- to middle-income apartments, and what areas will be developed as single-family houses. You'll want to be sure your laundry is in an area that will fit with the kinds of people who use laundromats—primarily low- to middle-income apartment-dwellers.

The Competition

Laundromats aren't like antique stores or boutique shops, which offer distinctive, specialty items. You may find these specialty stores in fairly close proximity to each other because shoppers like to browse several stores during one shopping trip. Laundromats, on the other hand, are like grocery stores. They're usually spaced apart every so many miles, since customers pretty much get the same results from each store.

Generally, you don't want to build a new laundromat near other laundromats. You also don't want to buy a laundromat that has too many competitors close by. If you do, the competition will be too intense, and you may end up dropping your prices so low you won't be able to get out of the red. As we mentioned in Chapter 1, the laundry business is a mature industry. Unless your region of the country is growing, it's likely there are already enough laundries in the neighborhood you're considering.

However, don't be too discouraged. If it seems like the laundry market is saturated in the area you're considering, be sure to take a good look at the competition. If the stores are run-down or located in high-crime areas,

Stat Fact

According to a recent survey by Ulrich Research Services, men are nearly twice as likely as women to do laundry at night. The survey results also show that most people prefer to do their wash on Saturday morning.

What's in a Name?

Traditionally, laundromats have been called just that—"Laundromat." Some are "Coin-Op Laundry," "Wash & Dry," or, in some Spanish-speaking areas, "Lavandería." While you want to make sure the name you give your laundry reflects the fact that it's a laundry, there's no reason you can't give your business more individuality.

Two partners we spoke to about choosing a name said, "We saw an opportunity to have a real identity." They named their laundry chain "Darcie's Laundry," after a friend. They didn't want to call their store simply, "Laundromat" or "Wash & Dry," and have customers say, "I'm going to go to that laundry that's across the street from the grocery store on the corner of 44th." They chose to spell the name with "ie" rather than "y" so they could incorporate their daisy logo—as the dot over the letter "i."

Another entrepreneur called her store "Busy Bee Laundry" because she wanted a name that could go with a whimsical logo. She chose the image of the busy bee to grace the T-shirts her attendants wear, as well as the signs inside the store.

many customers may be eager to visit a clean, new store—one with properly working equipment, a functioning change machine, and amenities such as computer terminals and free coffee. Also consider how many customers are using the store: If there's always a wait for machines, or the store is packed just before closing, there may be plenty of business to go around.

Finally, if you're offering different services from the competition, such as wash-and-fold, and the option to drop off and pick up dry cleaning, you may have a leg up on the competition. Craig H., the laundry owner in Washington state, opened all three of his laundries in locations that were near other laundromats. He said he didn't try to open stores near competitors, but that competition wasn't his only concern. "[We made] site selection based on a number of things: availability, traffic, rent, demographics," he said. "Having another laundry nearby is not something that we look for, but if the other ducks are all in a row, we'll try and analyze the space as the sum of its merits."

When you're choosing a location for your laundromat, consider nearby businesses. Busy people (and that's just about all of us) like to do their errands all at once. Having a drug store, a sandwich shop, a dry cleaner, and a supermarket near your location lets customers do everything in one fell swoop. They can pick up a sandwich for lunch, eat it while they do their laundry, then leave their dry cleaning with you, refill a prescription, and do the food shopping for the week—all without having to move the car.

Make sure the businesses surrounding your store are thriving and well kept. A shopping mall that's on the decline won't attract the traffic you need. And being near a string of run-down stores will make your laundromat look run-down as well. You should also steer clear of businesses that attract rowdy customers, such as bars or video arcades. Your customers may be scared away, and you'll likely have more of a problem with vandalism.

Hidden Competition

Keep in mind that some apartment buildings, especially larger complexes, have their own laundry facilities. If they are in good condition and offer enough machines, the residents will use those facilities.

If you think some of the apartment complexes near your potential site might already have washers and dryers, call them and find out. Larger apartment buildings (the ones most likely to have laundry facilities) usually have a rental office with a number listed in the phone book. When you call, don't forget to find out how many machines they have available for their renters. If they have just one or two washers, many of the residents will end up using a laundromat rather than wait for a machine to become available.

When there aren't enough machines, says Donovan, the residents aren't going to want to go down to the facility and wait for several other renters to do their laundry first. "At a laundromat, they can do all their wash at once. They feel more comfortable going to a place, getting five washers going, and getting all the wash done for the week."

Other Pieces of the Puzzle

Even if the demographics you have gathered seem favorable, and you've decided you can live with the competition, you may find yourself back at the drawing board if your location doesn't meet other important criteria. Other pieces of the puzzle, such as zoning requirements and lease agreements, have to fall into place for a location to be promising.

Zoned Out

The first step to take when you find a location you like is to check with the local municipality to ensure that it's zoned for a laundromat. If it's not, you're back to the drawing board—unless you can convince the local authority to change the zoning. If you have found an existing laundry that you want to buy, the previous owner should have checked this out already.

> **Smart Tip**
>
> Tip...
>
> The first step to take when you find a location you like is to check with the local municipality to ensure that it's zoned for a laundromat.

In addition to zoning requirements, you need to find out what fees you will have to pay for sewer connection (to hook up washers to sewer lines), and sewer and wastewater fees. As we'll discuss further in Chapter 5, sewer connection fees can be prohibitively expensive; however, they can also be applied sporadically, says Brian Wallace of the Coin Laundry Association. "On one side of the street there may be no impact fees, and down the block a little ways, there may be fees of several thousand dollars per washer," Wallace says. The only way to know what your fees will be like is to check with the local water district.

You'll also have to think about how difficult it will be to turn your leased space into a laundry, if it's not already one. You will need to make sure you have at least a two-inch connection for water and gas. You'll also need to check that the water service is metered. Making these upgrades can be expensive. Check with your distributor and your contractor (see Chapter 6 for more on experts) about the work that will need to be done to your site before it's ready to be a laundry. Your contractor will know what's needed to remodel the space and how much it will cost; your distributor will know what connections or utility requirements you will need for the equipment you plan to buy.

Lease, Lease, Lease

So you've determined that the location is good; the zoning allows a laundry at the site; the connection fees are low; and there are adequate water, gas, and electricity. You can stop saying, "location, location, location." Now you must start saying, "lease, lease, lease."

The importance of a good lease is second only to location. Rent will be one of your biggest expenses, so make sure the rent is something you can afford. Also remember that a laundry is not a consulting business, which can move offices frequently with little expense as long as the consultant has a cellular phone. As stated above, the success of a laundry is almost completely dependent on location. So if your landlord kicks you out of the building, all you have left is used equipment. And that's usually not worth more than a few thousand dollars.

> **Bright Idea**
>
> If your lease includes periodic rent increases, calculate what the rent will be for the last month you're there. Then do your best to project what your income will be at that time. Make sure you can still afford the rent at the end of the lease.

Beware!

If the site of your laundry-to-be is in a strip mall, you can expect to pay a share of the expenses for maintaining the common area. These can include fees for snow removal, landscaping, management, and taxes. Ask about these if you don't see them in the lease.

"You can't pick up and move a coin laundry," emphasizes Wallace. "Leases are very important. When the lease is over, you're out of business." So you'll need to negotiate a long lease—at least 10 years, 15 or 20 years if you can get it. If you're buying a laundromat, make sure that the lease is transferable and that you have at least ten years left on it. It's likely the landlord will raise the rent an expected amount, often according to inflation, so you can expect to pay more over the course of 20 years. That's OK as long as the increases are reasonable. You just want to make sure you won't be kicked out.

When you are drawing up the lease agreement, make sure you can have vending machines, food sales, or any other special services you plan to offer. Some leases may forbid ancillary income. Be especially careful about clauses that terminate the lease under special situations. These include fires or floods, or a life interest (this means that if the building owner dies, the lease is over).

Because the lease is so important to a laundromat, you should seek help from a real estate attorney when negotiating it. Certainly have an attorney review the lease before you sign it!

Park It Here

If you are looking at locations in a densely populated urban area, where people will be walking from their homes to the laundromat, you don't have to worry about parking. You can skip this section. However, if you're considering a suburban or rural location, you must pay close attention. It is vitally important for your store to have adequate parking. We are back to that convenience thing—if it's not easy to park the car, customers are not going to use your laundry.

Many suburban laundry owners find themselves operating a store in a strip mall. A large part of the reason is that strip malls have plenty of parking. But don't just look at the parking lot in the middle of the weekday and figure there's plenty of room. Drive into the parking lot during the laundry rush hours—evenings and weekends—and see how easily you can find a parking space. If you have to wait 15 minutes before you can pull your car into a spot, you can bet your customers will drive off to another laundry long before 15 minutes are up.

Also think about how accessible a potential site is from the road. If your future customers have to make a left turn into heavy traffic without a protected signal, they may drive on. And if they have to risk their lives to pull out of the parking lot, they'll try another store next time.

See and Be Seen

While you need to make sure your customers can drive or walk easily to your laundromat, you must also be sure that passersby can see it. A spot in an alley with good parking might work for a hairdresser who gets most of her business through referrals, but it won't work for laundry owners.

Most customers find laundromats because they see them on the street. They find them when they're walking to the grocery store or driving to work, and they decide to give them a try. While word-of-mouth and advertising will also help to draw in customers, visibility is probably your best advertisement. Make sure the site you're investigating can be seen easily from the road. Drive or walk by it from different directions and at different times of the day, and note how easily it stands out.

If your potential site is in a suburban or rural area, you'll likely do better if the site is on a busy street rather than a quiet, out-of-the-way road. In urban areas, where there is plenty of foot traffic, you'll want to think more about a central location that will draw residents from the immediate vicinity. A corner spot is often helpful because people can see your store from more than one street.

Check with the municipality where you will open your laundry to find out about signage regulations. Cities and counties have different rules about how big signs can be and whether lighting is allowed. Also check with your landlord: Strip malls and business complexes may have rules regarding signs, too.

In general, the larger and brighter your sign is, the better. You should try not to clutter signs with too many words or phrases. And make sure the words "laundry," "laundromat," or "wash" are included in your sign so there's no danger of customers mistaking your store for another type of business.

Tip...

Smart Tip

Sign research has shown that certain colors are easier to read at a distance. The top five color combinations (in order of the easiest to read):

1. Black letters on yellow background
2. Black letters on white background
3. Yellow letters on black background
4. White letters on blue background
5. Yellow letters on blue background

On a Mission

Once you've decided to pursue the laundry business and have found a suitable location, be sure to write a mission statement to help guide you in designing and developing your store. A mission statement is a brief description of your

Developing Your Mission Statement

Use this worksheet to start developing your mission statement. Your statement should clearly define the following:

- ❍ *Your geographic area.* From what area do you expect to draw customers?
- ❍ *Your customers.* What types of customers will use your laundromat—students, seniors, vacationers, families?
- ❍ *The services you will offer.* Will you provide wash-and-fold, alterations, manicures, or any other services?
- ❍ *The image you want to project.* What kind of atmosphere will you provide for your customers? Will you have a theme, such as "The Old West" or "Outer Space," for your laundry? Do you want to be known as the largest laundry in town, the laundry with friendly attendants, or the laundry that's fun to visit?

Mission Statement for

____

(your business name)

____
____
____
____
____
____
____
____
____
____
____
____
____
____
____

business's purpose. It should include what region your business serves, who your customers are and what services you will offer.

For example, one mission statement might be, "Our mission is to provide a fun, safe and clean location for Tallahassee residents to wash their clothes." Or: "Our mission is to offer a store with enough quality laundry equipment for southwest Portland residents to be able to do their laundry quickly and at a fair price."

An accurate mission statement helps you focus as you grow your business, and it helps your employees understand their work goals. Print the statement in large type on a poster and display it in a place where you and your attendants will see it every day. Take a look at the worksheet we've provided on page 32 for developing an effective mission statement.

In addition to finding your customers and a good location, you have yet another major decision to make—will you buy an existing laundromat or build a new one in a leased space? In Chapter 4, we will show you how to approach this question and make the best choice for your new business.

4

To Buy or Build?

One of the first decisions you'll have to make when you join the laundry owners' club is whether you want to buy an existing laundry business or build a new one in a leased storefront. Your decision will be based partly on personal preference. Do you want to take a risk on a new, untried store? Or do you want to take over one with a proven track

Photo Courtesy: The Last Load

record? It's very likely, however, that market conditions will determine which route you choose. In this chapter, we'll help you decide when it's right to build a laundromat and when it makes more sense to buy an existing one. We'll also steer you through the buying process.

When to Build

Most laundry owners who build a laundromat do so by leasing a storefront, remodeling the space, and installing equipment—rather than constructing a store from the ground up. So when is building a new laundromat the best choice?

As we've mentioned, most areas of the country have all the laundromats they need. However, there are cities and counties that are growing rapidly and potentially need new laundromats. If the population growth in an area includes an increase in the customer base that most often uses laundries (low- to middle-income renters), building a new laundromat might make more sense than buying one.

Areas experiencing a population boom aren't the only places in need of a laundromat, though. There are also a few neighborhoods that just don't have one. Either the laundromat business never made it there, or a laundry closed. Dave and Kris A., who own a laundry in New Glarus, Wisconsin, opened their business several years after the laundromat in their town shut down. Everyone knew the town needed a new laundry.

> **Smart Tip**
> Ask to see the general plan for your city or county. This will have information on how much the area is expected to grow, where it will grow, and what type of housing will be built.

"It became kind of a hot topic around here," Dave says. "Two other people were thinking about doing it. It was a race to see who bought the land and was first." Whatever the situation in your town, just make sure there are enough customers to support your business.

Another reason you might take a chance on building a new laundromat is if you think your business can draw customers from existing laundromats. Maybe you have a new gimmick you want to promote, such as a combination nightclub/laundry; perhaps you will offer a variety of services, such as wash-and-fold, dry cleaning, or clothing repair. Or you may plan to build a large laundry with plenty of machines, a children's play area, televisions, and a snack bar. If the laundries in your neighborhood are small and offer no amenities, customers may choose your business over the competition because their stay will be more pleasant and they won't have to wait for machines.

If you decide to go this route, your decision should be based on solid market research and not just a hunch. Find out if there is a sufficient customer base from which to draw business, and whether they want the atmosphere or amenities that you will offer.

Your decision to build rather than buy may depend on what's for sale. If the laundries for sale in your area have too many problems, or if none are for sale, building may be your only option—provided that your area can support a new laundry.

Finally, you may want to build if you feel uncomfortable taking over a business. Buying an existing laundry is a little like buying a used car—you're never really sure why the owner is selling. In addition, you don't know what kinds of problems you may inherit if you take over somebody's lease.

Building 101

If you decide to build a store, you'll need to negotiate a lease, hire a contractor, choose a distributor, and promote the store. Your distributor should be able to tell you if you've found a good location for your laundry. We'll cover the basics of choosing contractors and distributors in Chapter 6.

> **Beware!**
> If you're building a laundry, be aware that regular insurance covering property and casualty will not cover you during the construction phase. To cover yourself in case of fire, theft, or other damage while you're building your store, purchase builders' risk insurance.

Keep in mind that if you decide to build a laundromat, you will have an advantage over your competitors if you build a much larger store. Although your competition can often add amenities, such as wash-and-fold service or televisions, they can't add to the size of their store. This means they can't compete with the number of machines you'll have, and they likely can't add a snack bar or offer services that take up space, such as dry-cleaning drop-off and pickup. "It makes sense to build if you put in a nice big new laundry," says Lionel Bogut, a consultant and laundry owner. "People know they can always come to your store and find a washer."

Craig H., who opened laundries in three cities in Washington state, found that his chain has done very well by drawing customers looking for nicer equipment and more amenities. The chain offers a kids' play area, many televisions, full-time attendants, and a card system. "It seemed like in our area there was an opportunity for larger, more exciting stores," he says.

When to Buy

There are several good reasons to consider buying an existing laundry business rather than building a new one. If there isn't the customer base for another laundry in your town, or your water district imposes such high sewer connection fees that it's not practical to build, buying an existing laundry may be your only option.

How Big Can You Go?

You may be motivated to build a huge store to make a bigger profit or to draw in customers who don't want to wait for machines at smaller stores. Just remember that a big store is going to cost you—not only in construction costs and the price of equipment, but also in the rent you will have to pay to keep the machines waiting around to be used.

If you're in a large metropolitan area with good access to low- and middle-income rental housing, you can probably get away with a large store. Customers will skip other laundries to visit yours if it's large and has a pleasant atmosphere. But if the customer base you expect to draw from is small, you need to be sure you don't build any larger than necessary.

If your store is the only laundry in a small town, for example, there will be a limited demand for your business. Customers aren't likely to drive 30 miles from the next town, no matter how nice your store is. You'll have to determine how much laundry you can expect your customers to bring in and size your store accordingly. Start by reviewing a demographics report for your area. Then discuss what an appropriate size might be for your store with your distributor or consultant.

In some areas of the country, sewer connection fees are as high as $8,000 per washer. So, if you build a 40-washer laundromat, you'll have to pay more than $300,000 just for the installation of your washers. These fees can double the price of building a new laundromat, making it far more attractive to buy an existing one instead.

Finally, you might choose to buy a laundromat if you don't want the hassle of starting a business from scratch and worrying about whether it will take off. An existing store is already up and running, and it has a proven track record.

If You Buy

Possibly the most important factor you'll need to consider when buying a laundry business is where it's located. As we discussed in Chapter 3, there are many factors that will go into finding just the right location. Your laundry must be close to the homes of its likely customers—low- to middle-income renters—and you must be able to negotiate a long lease at a good price. It should be far enough removed from the competition, unless your business will have an edge on the competition. You should also consider a site that is visible to potential customers, easy to renovate (if that's your plan), and in a place where you can provide good parking.

You can find laundries for sale in the newspaper. Many distributors (the people who sell you equipment) also act as brokers. They'll sell a laundry to you on behalf of the owner. Distributors will also build new laundries themselves and sell them to new owners. They'll develop a property, install the equipment, and add all the extras, such as seats and laundry carts. Then they'll work out the expenses and expected income for the store, and give that to you in a sheet called a pro forma (to see an example, turn

A Better Way to Go

You won't have to worry about a lease that will expire, a landlord who's particular about changes, or any common-area expenses when you own the property your laundry is on. While it's not a requirement, there are advantages to this strategy if you can swing it.

Dave A., who owns a laundromat in New Glarus, Wisconsin, with his wife, Kris, bought a piece of land in town and built a laundry on the property. He had to get a loan to pay for it, but he never has to worry about getting kicked out or about rent hikes.

Unfortunately, this tactic won't work for every laundry owner. Some of the best places to locate a laundry—such as strip malls—aren't for sale or are prohibitively expensive.

to pages 41 through 43). If you decide to buy a new laundromat from a distributor, don't take the distributor's word for it. You still need to research the location carefully. Remember, it's in the best interest of the distributor to sell you the store.

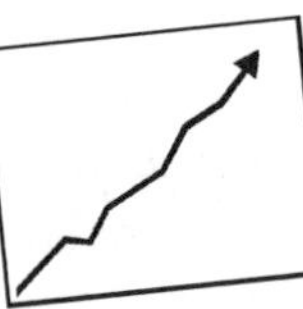

Stat Fact

How long before laundry equipment needs replacing? Top-loaders will last between five and eight years, and front-loaders will last from 10 to 15 years. Dryers will give you 15 to 20 years before they give up the ghost. And water heating systems and change machines will live for about 10 to 15 years.

Kicking the Tires

Once you have found a laundromat you're interested in buying, you'll need to investigate it as if you were buying a used car: look under the hood, check the mileage, and research the model. Find out why the owner wants to sell; if there's a good reason, you need to know what it is upfront. "They always have a story," says Robert G., who has purchased three laundries in New York state.

If you're buying from a distributor, remember that he or she is trying to make a sale, not give you a great business opportunity. "New people need to be very cautious because it's in the distributor's best interest to sell the store," says Janet H., who has purchased eight laundries in Southern California, mostly from distributors. The most important step is to make sure there is a customer base to support the laundry. The second thing is to determine the length of the lease on the laundry. If the owner has two years left on the lease, you know why he or she is selling—the business will be closed in two years. You'll want at least 10 years on the lease. Ask to see a copy of the lease agreement.

Next, check with your city or county government about any construction slated for the neighborhood. Make sure there aren't any upcoming changes that would make the owner want to sell. A large new laundry chain next door could kill your business. So could a plan to raze the apartment complexes across the street and build high-end condominiums. You should also obtain current demographic information. Is the number of renters in the area stagnant or decreasing? Maybe that's why the owner is selling.

Take a tour of the store you are considering buying so you can see firsthand what sort of shape it's in. Call the owner of the store to arrange a time. Take a careful look over the "Prepurchase Laundry Evaluation" worksheet we've provided on page 46 to see what you'll need to inspect to cover all your bases.

First look at the parking situation to see if customers have enough places to park. Then look in the customer area to get an overall impression of the store. Check whether any major repairs are needed for damaged floors, walls, or ceilings. Think about the layout of the store: Is there enough room for customers to move laundry carts around? Is it open and visible from the street so vandals or thieves can't hide? Would it be possible to do some inexpensive renovating to improve the store?

Pro Forma

				Vend Price			Vend Price
Customer Name:		Top-load washers	20	1.00	35 lb. FL washers	0	0.00
Laundry Name:	Launderland	18 lb. FL washers	0	0.00	50 lb. FL washers	8	3.75
Laundry Address:	123 Spotless Blvd.	27 lb. FL washers	14	2.00	80 lb. FL washers	2	5.00
Laundry City:	Cleantown, CA	30 lb. Slimline dryers	0	0.00	30 lb. Stacked dryers	22	0.25/10

Average turns a day for top-load washer	3.0	Percentage of dryer revenue to washer revenue	40%
Average turns a day for front-load washer	6.0	Average total income a day	655.00

REVENUE	Monthly	Year 1	Year 2	Year 3	Year 4	Year 5	Year 6	Year 7
Washers and dryers	19,923	239,075	248,638	258,584	279,684	290,871	302,506	314,606
Vending (soap, drinks, snacks)	1,790	21,480	22,339	23,233	24,162	25,129	26,134	27,179
Vending commissions	300	3,600	3,744	3,894	4,050	4,211	4,380	4,555
Wash-and-fold	0	0	0	0	0	0	0	0
TOTAL INCOME	22,013	264,155	274,721	285,710	297,138	309,024	321,385	334,240

Pro Forma, continued

EXPENSES	Per ft.	Sq. ft.	Monthly	Year 1	Year 2	Year 3	Year 4	Year 5	Year 6	Year 7
Occupancy cost:										
Base rent:	1.15	2,450	2,818	33,810	33,810	35,010	36,210	36,210	38,610	38,610
Taxes:	0.14		343	4,116	4,281	4,452	4,630	4,815	5,008	5,208
Insurance:	0.08		196	2,352	2,446	2,544	2,646	2,752	2,862	2,976
CAM:	0.03		74	882	917	954	992	1.032	1.073	1.116
Gas @	10.00%		1.992	23.908	24,864	25,858	26,893	27,968	29,087	30,251
Water @	11.50%		2,291	27,494	28,593	29,737	30,927	32,164	33,450	34,788
Electric @	5.00%		996	11,954	12,432	12,929	13,446	13,984	14,544	15,125
Insurance			400	4,800	4,922	5,192	5,399	5,615	5,840	6,074
Personal P. tax			340	4,080	4,080	4,080	4,080	4,080	4,080	4,080
Trash collection			100	1,200	1,248	1,298	1,350	1,404	1,460	1,518
Vending costs			895	10,740	11,170	11,616	12,081	12,564	13,067	13,590
Labor—$5.75 an hour/84 hours a week			2,512	30,139	31.345	32,599	33,903	35,259	36,669	38,136
Parts and repairs (3-year warranty)			199	2,391	2,486	5,172	5,379	8,391	11.635	12,100
Wash-and-fold			0	0	0	0	0	0	0	0
Miscellaneous			220	2,642	2,747	2,857	2,971	3,090	3,214	3,342
TOTAL EXPENSES			13,376	160,506	165,411	174,298	180,906	189,327	200,598	206,914
CASH FLOW			8,637	103,649	109,310	111,412	116,232	119,696	120,787	127,326

Pro Forma, continued

DEBT SERVICE ANALYSIS					
Total sale price	474,490	Financing term	84 months	Equipment, freight, tax	265,190
Down payment (35%)	166,072	Financing rate	10.75% variable	Construction, plans, sign	209,300
Finance balance	308,419	Monthly debt service	5,240.43	Utilities fees	0

CASH FLOW ANALYSIS	Year 1	Year 2	Year 3	Year 4	Year 5	Year 6	Year 7
Monthly cash flow from operations	8,637	9,109	9,284	9,686	9,975	10,066	10,611
Annual cash flow from operations	103,649	109,310	111,412	116,232	119,696	120,787	127,326
Less annual debt service	(62,885)	(62,885)	(62,885)	(62,885)	(62,885)	(62,885)	(62,885)
Net cash flow after debt service	40,764	46,425	48,527	53,347	56,811	57,902	64,441

TAXABLE INCOME/LOSS ANALYSIS	Year 1	Year 2	Year 3	Year 4	Year 5	Year 6	Year 7
Cash flow before debt service	103,649	109,310	111,412	116,232	119,696	120,787	127,326
Depreciation	(67,986)	(107,995)	(65,319)	(39,713)	(39,713)	(20,509)	(1,304)
Interest	(31,646)	(28,117)	(24,189)	(19,818)	(14,954)	(9,539)	(3,514)
Taxable income/loss	4,017	(26,801)	21,904	56,701	65,030	90,739	122,508

RETURN ON INVESTMENT ANALYSIS	Year 1	Year 2	Year 3	Year 4	Year 5	Year 6	Year 7
Cash on cash R.O.I.	0.25	0.28	0.29	0.32	0.34	0.35	0.39
Equity build-up R.O.I.	0.19	0.21	0.23	0.26	0.29	0.32	0.36
Total return on investment	0.43	0.49	0.53	0.58	0.63	0.67	0.75

All income and expense calculations are projected to increase 4 percent annually. PWS Inc. makes a good faith effort to project future income and expenses but does not guarantee this pro forma and is not responsible for its accuracy. The R.O.I. analysis does not consider the tax consequence when the business is sold.

> **Smart Tip**
> To keep customers from sitting on machines and folding tables, you should provide chairs where they can sit and wait for their laundry to finish.

Look in the back rooms where the water heaters and storage areas are. Go behind the dryers; check out the restroom. You'll want to make sure the store is well kept, even in the areas customers never see. These areas should be neat and free of lint buildup and water stains. If the owner can't keep the back areas in good condition, he or she may not be keeping the machines in good working order either.

This brings us to an important part of the inspection: Check the machines carefully to see that they're in good condition. If more than a few are broken, this shows that the owner is not keeping up with repairs—or that the machines are of poor quality. Ask the owner for documents stating the age of the equipment; don't just take his or her word for it. We've provided a list of "Warning Signs" on this page that you should look out for when you tour a prospective laundry business.

If you're new to the laundry business, it's a good idea to bring along someone experienced to evaluate the condition of the store. You can hire a consultant to give you an honest evaluation (see Chapter 6 for more on consultants and other experts). You can also ask another laundry owner to accompany you, or you can approach your regional laundry association for assistance.

Warning Signs Checklist

If you're considering buying a laundromat, the current owner is likely to paint a rosy picture of the store's condition. So you should inspect the store yourself and take note of any of the following warning signs:

- ❒ Cracked floor tiles or other damage to the floor
- ❒ Signs of vandalism to coin boxes or change machines
- ❒ More than a few machines out of order
- ❒ Water stains around washers
- ❒ Give in the drums of dryers and front-loaders
- ❒ Black dryer drums (indicating the coating has worn off)
- ❒ Burn or smoke marks in access doors of dryers
- ❒ Discoloration or burn marks on water heater
- ❒ Rust or discoloration of water heater exhaust ducts
- ❒ Water marks or water on the floor near the water heater
- ❒ Malfunctioning bill changer
- ❒ Vandalism in restroom

Crunching the Numbers

Once you've evaluated the condition of the store and its equipment, you must find out how much the store is making. Again, don't take the owner's word for it. Ask for the following documents so that you can evaluate the expenses involved in running the store:

- The lease agreement (to see amount of the rent and scheduled increases)
- Water bills
- Gas bills
- Electric bills
- Sewer bills
- Repair bills
- Employee payroll
- Insurance agreement
- Annual taxes
- Invoices for supplies

Don't forget the myriad of other expenses you incur while running a business, such as trash removal, office supplies, advertising, telephone charges, cleaning supplies, association fees, and accounting.

Once you have a handle on expenses, you'll want to evaluate how much income the store generates. You know how much each customer pays to use a machine, so all you need to know is how often they are used. The owner will tell you how many turns a day the machines get (the number of times each machine is used daily), but try to verify this figure by getting a few outside opinions. An experienced laundry owner, distributor or consultant—someone who doesn't have a stake in selling you the store—may be able to tell you how many turns a day you can expect. Another option is to visit the store yourself to see how many times each machine gets used.

Robert G. said that when he found a store he was interested in, he would spend an entire day in the store and count the number of times each machine was used. "I took a day out of my week, and I sat there with a pad and paper and charted out each time a machine was used. I did that on a slow day like a Wednesday or a Thursday, and I multiplied that by 365 to give myself

Bright Idea

One way to determine how much money a laundry is taking in is to calculate the number of turns a day (the number of times a machine is used daily) based on water usage. Top-loaders and front-loaders of various sizes use a predictable amount of water. Contact the California Coin Laundry Association to learn how to make this calculation (see the Appendix for contact information).

Prepurchase Laundry Evaluation

When you take a tour of a laundromat for sale, take this worksheet and write down your impressions. These notes—along with the length of the lease, age of the equipment, and demographics—will help you determine what the laundromat is worth.

Parking: ______________________________

____

Visibility from street: ______________________________

____

Condition of floor: ______________________________

____

Condition of ceiling: ______________________________

____

Appearance of washers: ______________________________

____

Appearance of dryers: ______________________________

____

Washer-dryer ratio: ______________________________

____

Condition of vending machines: ______________________________

____

Condition of change machines: ______________________________

____

Layout of equipment: ______________________________

____

Condition of back rooms: ______________________________

____

Amenities: ______________________________

____

Temperature inside store: ______________________________

____

Overall atmosphere: ______________________________

____

Number of customers: ______________________________

____

a rough average of what the store is taking in," he says. "That's worth a day out of your week if you're interested in a store."

Robert's count will be low, of course, because more laundry gets washed on the weekends. But this count will give you a general idea of what kind of income to expect. See the income and expense analyses in Chapter 11 for more on figuring out a store's net income.

What's It Worth to You?

Once you have crunched the numbers and decided that the laundromat is making a heady enough profit, you'll need to determine whether the asking price is fair. This can be difficult because the value of a laundromat is subjective. A laundry may be worth more to you than to someone else because you own the sandwich shop next door and would like to merge them. On the other hand, you may be looking at several stores and have only so much money to spend; so you might not be willing to pay as much as other buyers.

Whatever your situation, you still don't want to overpay. There's no need to shell out $300,000 when a laundry is worth only $200,000. So how do you determine a fair value for a laundromat? Some laundry owners figure that the value of a laundry is roughly equal to 50 times its monthly net income. So if a laundry is taking in $1,000

The Fixer-Upper

You may be able to find a good deal on a laundromat that has fallen into disrepair. If the owner hasn't kept the store neat and the machines in good condition, it's likely that customers have started to drift elsewhere. This reduces profits and in turn lowers the laundromat's value. With a little tender, loving care, you may be able to attract customers back to the store and turn the business around.

Robert G., who has purchased three laundromats in New York state, says he looks for laundries that need a little spiffing up—new paint, new floors, a few new machines—but not major repairs. "Those are usually the best ones," he says. "You don't want something too run-down, with pipes cracking and stuff falling down."

Janet H., who has purchased eight laundries in Southern California, says that she can lift a sagging store by adding more lighting, applying a fresh coat of paint and keeping it clean. "If you don't improve your store, keep it clean and paint it; [otherwise] people are going to go elsewhere," she says.

> **Beware!**
> Laundry income peaks at certain times of the year. The first warm weather in the spring and the first cold weather in the fall, result in an increase in business by as much as 20 percent. Be sure you adjust for this if you're evaluating a laundry during those times of the year.

per month after expenses, it's worth $50,000. This amount assumes that the lease has 15 years left, the equipment is three years old, the neighborhood is stable, and the pricing and amenities are average. For more favorable conditions—a longer lease, a growing population of renters, new equipment—you should assume that the laundry is worth more than the estimate based on the standard assumptions. Likewise, for unfavorable conditions, such as machines in need of repair, low prices, and fewer amenities, you should assume that the store is worth less than the estimate.

This rule of thumb can give you a basic idea of the value, but be aware that many other conditions can affect the price of a laundry business. The cost of land in your area, high sewer connection fees, and competition from other laundries all figure into the value.

If you're in a metropolitan area, you can compare the selling prices of similar laundromats, much like real estate agents do with houses. If a laundry that's the same size as the one you're looking at sells for $150,000 in a comparable neighborhood, you can expect to pay about that amount.

However, because the value of a laundromat depends on so many factors—lease, location, equipment, and demographics, to name a few—it's best to seek advice from someone who has experience. A consultant or another laundry owner who's been in the business for a while can help you, as can a distributor. Just make sure the person you're seeking advice from is not going to profit from the sale.

Laundry consultant Lionel Bogut says that he once reviewed a laundromat with an asking price of $500,000. The potential buyers asked him to determine whether that was a fair price. He looked over the profits and expenses, the state of the equipment, and the conditions of the lease, and decided that the laundry was worth between $200,000 and $220,000. Eventually, the owner dropped the price. "The [buyers] saved themselves a lot of money," he says.

5

Financial Figuring

So you like the idea of opening a laundry. It suits your working style and personality, and you understand the steps you need to take to research the market. The next step—and it's a crucial one—is to crunch the numbers. Before you plunge headfirst into the laundromat business, you must know how much cash you will need upfront and how much you can expect to make.

In this chapter we'll give you a rough idea of start-up costs and how to find the money to finance your business. Later, in Chapter 11, we'll walk you through the process of figuring out your projected net income.

Start-Up Costs

You can expect to encounter a number of basic start-up costs in order to get into the laundry business. Depending on whether you build a new laundry in a leased space or buy an existing one, your costs will include:

- Market research (literature, subscriptions, association fees)
- The cost of an existing laundry business
- Construction or remodeling (if you are building a new laundromat)
- Washer hook-up fees (sewer connection)
- Licenses and permits
- Equipment (see the "Equipment Basics" checklist on page 53)

Keep in mind that if you buy a laundry, you don't pay for licenses or sewer connection fees (unless you decide to have additional washers installed). You'll have to pay for renovation and any new equipment you decide to install if you want to update the laundry.

In addition to these basic start-up costs, you will also have a number of ongoing expenses—a subject we will return to in Chapter 11. These include:

- Lease or rental costs
- Utilities (gas, sewer, water, and electric)
- Insurance (fire, theft, and liability)
- Employee payroll and benefits
- Miscellaneous supplies (cleaning supplies, soap, invoices for wash-and-fold, bathroom supplies, etc.)

Research and Development

If you're new to the laundry business, you will need to spend some time getting to know it better. That includes reading everything you can on the subject, including current publications, as well as previous issues of trade magazines and newsletters. It will also be important for you to join professional associations and to interview experienced laundry owners. While we can't put a figure on the time you'll spend conducting research, you can count on spending about $300 to $400 for literature and association fees.

Once you've completed your research, you will need to figure out how much it will cost to build your store—to remodel a space and fill it with laundry equipment—or to buy an existing laundry. Whether you decide to buy or build, you can expect to pay between $200,000 and $500,000 for an average-size laundromat (about 2,000 square feet).

If you're buying an existing laundry, figuring out your major start-up costs is simple—just determine the value of the business. (See Chapter 4 to learn more about arriving at a fair price for a laundry.) If you plan to renovate the existing store by painting the interior or putting in new flooring, be sure to add these costs to your start-up expenses.

If you decide to build, figuring out your start-up costs involves a little more work. Since you'll be leasing a space that was something other than a laundry in a previous life, the cost of the construction is going to depend on how much remodeling you have to do. If the space you've chosen was formerly a beauty salon, for example, you're going to have to add enough water, sewer, and gas pipes for the conversion to a laundry. You'll also have to provide enough electrical outlets, possibly move a few walls, and completely redecorate before it will look like a laundromat. You should hire a contractor to help you do all this remodeling (we'll return to this subject in Chapter 6).

In general, you can expect to pay between $100,000 and $250,000 for the construction costs to remodel an average-size space (2,000 square feet). This includes the cost of installing your equipment and putting in folding tables and seating. The remainder of your major start-up costs will be buying the equipment itself.

Be aware that your construction costs can fluctuate due to factors like the one that Brian D., the laundry owner in Iowa City, describes. When he was negotiating a lease for his laundry, he tried to get a spot on the end of a strip mall. He failed: He lost it to a woman who wanted to open a deli. So his contractor had to figure out a way to duct the dryers out the back and up into the ceiling. If he'd had the end spot, the ducts could have been placed out the side instead, and he would have saved on construction costs.

Licenses and Hidden Fees

The licenses and permits you will need depends entirely on your location. Check with your municipality regarding the following:

- Business license
- Health department license (if you are serving food)
- Fire department permit
- Air-and-water pollution control permit
- Sign permit
- Public improvement fees
- Impact fees

"Be sure to do [this research] ahead of time," says Craig H., the laundry owner in Washington state.

> Tip...
>
> **Smart Tip**
>
> Check with the Small Business Administration office in your state to find out what sort of licenses and permits you'll need. Some states publish a book that can walk you through the process. Look under "State Government" in your phone book.

You should also be aware of a few lesser-known fees that will affect you as a laundry owner. In many areas around the country, municipal water districts charge sewer connection fees. These can cost you anywhere from $200 to $8,000 per washer. If the fees are $8,000 per washer, the owner of a laundry with 30 washers must pay $240,000 in hook-up fees—almost what he'll pay for construction! Brian Wallace, of the Coin Laundry Association, tells us that high hook-up fees are one of the biggest problems facing the coin laundry industry today. These fees are a major challenge to laundry developers. In areas where operators are forced to pay these fees, the price of laundromats has also risen dramatically. If the fees are high in your chosen area, you may need to reconsider your entire plan.

In addition to sewer connection fees, you may find that you have to pay sewer and waste water fees, too—check with the local municipality. Don't neglect to check on these charges when you're researching a laundry business. After all, you will be using these utilities heavily, so you'll want to know if the monthly charges will be manageable from the get-go.

The Goods

If you decide to buy a laundry, you will already have a full complement of equipment—unless you want to replace a few of the older machines or add a few more machines to meet customer demand. However, if you decide to build a laundry, buying equipment will eat up virtually all the rest of your start-up costs. You can expect to pay between $100,000 and $250,000 to fill an average-size laundromat with washers and dryers. Refer to the checklist of "Equipment Basics" on page 53 as you read through our rundown of equipment to buy for your new laundry.

Top-load washers cost between $750 and $1,000 each, and front-load washers cost between $3,000 and $6,000 each, depending on their size. One stacked dryer (which means two dryers arranged one on top of the other in a joined cabinet casing) costs between $4,000 and $5,000. You will also need a warranty to cover all the equipment you buy. A three-year warranty on parts and service, which you purchase from the equipment manufacturer, will be $2,000 to $6,000—this will cover all your equipment.

If you want to add a card system, it will cost you in the neighborhood of $20,000 to $30,000, including readers on the machines, a card dispenser, and cards. The software that computes equipment usage (which machine was used, the time of day, and the turns a day for each type of equipment) will run about $6,000 to $10,000. But take heart: With a card system, you don't have to buy a change machine, which runs in the ballpark of $1,000 to $3,000. For more information on card systems, see Chapter 7.

A water heating system will run you between $5,000 and $15,000, and a soap vending machine will cost between $500 and $1,500. Those laundry carts that let customers transport their clothes from washer to dryer cost $75 to $100 each. Supplies such as soap, cleaning equipment, signs, clocks, and trash cans should run another $750 to $1,000.

If you plan to offer wash-and-fold service, you will need a cash register, laundry scale, and counter where customers can pick up their laundry. A basic electronic cash register will run you about $600. A scale for weighing wash-and-fold laundry will cost you between $400 and $1,000. The cost of a counter should be covered under your construction/installation costs.

If you want to buy a snack or soda vending machine, it will cost you between $3,000 and $4,000. As an alternative, you could contract with a vending company: They pay for the machine and the snacks and sodas, and split the profits with you.

If you choose to add amenities, such as televisions or computers for your customers to play on the Internet, this will cost you, too. A television will run you about $200 to

Equipment Basics Checklist

Store essentials:

- ❒ Top-load washers
- ❒ Front-load washers
- ❒ Dryers
- ❒ Warranty on parts and service
- ❒ Water heating system
- ❒ Soap vending machine
- ❒ Change machines
- ❒ Laundry carts
- ❒ Folding tables
- ❒ Seats
- ❒ Miscellaneous supplies (soap, cleaning supplies, signs, clock, trash cans, bathroom supplies)

For wash-and-fold:

- ❒ Counter
- ❒ Cash register
- ❒ Scale (for weighing laundry)
- ❒ Invoices

Office supplies:

- ❒ Computer
- ❒ Software
- ❒ Phone with answering machine
- ❒ Calculator
- ❒ Business stationery/cards

Optional items:

- ❒ Automatic lock system
- ❒ Timer for lights
- ❒ Televisions/computers
- ❒ Snack or soda vending machines
- ❒ Video security system

$500, and a basic computer system will cost you in the neighborhood of $2,000. Also factor in monthly fees for an Internet service provider, around $20 to $25.

Finally, if you don't hire attendants, you might want to install a video security system. This will cost you at least $1,500 depending on the number of cameras and type of equipment you want. We said it would cost you.

Other Equipment

You'll also need invoices to give to customers who drop off their laundry for wash-and-fold. You can buy basic invoices from an office supply store, or you can have special ones printed up with your store's name and policies.

If your laundry will be attended, you'll want a phone in the store. It should have an answering machine or a voice-mail service. You're looking at paying $70 to $80 for a basic two-line speakerphone with auto-redial, memory, and a mute button. To install a phone line in your store, it will cost you approximately $40 to $60. Expect to pay another $40 to $150 for an answering machine—or get voice mail for just $6 to $20 a month.

Consider buying a cellular phone or pager if you'll be away from your laundry much of the time and your attendants or customers will need to get a hold of you quickly. If you will have an unattended laundry without a phone, and you plan to take care of your office work at home, you may want to consider installing a separate business line so you can be listed in the Yellow Pages.

Like any other small-business owner, you'll need equipment to run administrative tasks—paying bills, managing finances, calling repair people. A computer is not essential, although it will make charting equipment use and keeping track of finances much easier. If you don't already have one, you can purchase a basic set-up for $2,000 to $4,000 dollars, including a hard drive, monitor, modem, and printer. A spreadsheet program such as Microsoft Excel, or accounting software such as Intuit QuickBooks, will save you a lot of time. Expect to pay in the range of $60 to $220 for one of these programs.

You will probably need to copy a few documents and fax a few letters, but it's not likely to happen often enough to justify purchasing a copier or a fax machine. You will, however, need a good calculator for figuring out your income and expenses; this will cost anywhere from $15 to $50, depending on the model you pick.

Tip...

Smart Tip

The Coin Laundry Association offers tours of laundromats. This is a great opportunity for prospective laundry owners to see how different laundries are set up and run. Tour participants also have a chance to talk with successful owners. See the Appendix for information on how to contact the Coin Laundry Association.

Business stationery is not essential, as you won't be writing letters to prospective clients, but it's convenient for writing letters to suppliers or repair companies. And you may want to buy business cards that you can pass out to prospective customers.

For Example...

On page 56, we've provided a sample "Start-Up Costs" worksheet for two hypothetical companies: Suds-Are-Us, a large laundry with attendants and wash-and-fold service; and Squeaky Clean Wash-and-Dry, a smaller laundry with no attendants and fewer amenities.

The owner of Suds-Are-Us built his new laundry in a 3,000-square-foot space that he rented in a strip mall. The construction costs associated with remodeling the space and converting it to a laundry cost him $300,000. He bought the following equipment and had it installed: 30 top-load washers, 12 25-pound front-load washers, three 50-pound front-loaders, and 16 stacked dryers (32 dryers total). Including the water heating system, a card system with software, and a soap vending machine, his equipment cost him a total of $194,500. On top of this, the local utility district charges $500 to hook up each washer, so the owner had to pay a total of $22,500 to have all 45 washing machines hooked up. He also had to pay $6,000 for a parts and service warranty on his new equipment.

Suds-Are-Us has three employees and offers customers wash-and-fold service (with the associated costs of a cash register and laundry scale). A computer and three

Getting off the Ground

Industry experts say a laundry takes between six months and a year to start turning a profit. "After that, you grow," says laundry consultant Lionel Bogut. "And you continue to grow as long as you take care of your customers and your equipment."

Collette C., who owns a laundry in Evans, Colorado, says she and her partner, Kim C., were "out of the red" in three months, and their business is still growing. On the other hand, Dave and Kris A., with a laundromat in New Glarus, Wisconsin, have been in business just over a year and are now breaking even. "Our goal is to get the equipment paid for as fast as we can," Dave says. His costs are a little higher than many other laundry owners because he purchased the property on which his store is located.

Start-Up Costs

Compare these start-up costs for our two hypothetical businesses: the newly built Suds-Are-Us and Squeaky Clean, an existing laundry that the owner bought and renovated.

Start-Up Expenses	Suds-Are-Us	Squeaky Clean
Cost of existing laundry business	$0	$150,000
Construction/remodeling (new laundry)	$300,000	$0
Renovations (to existing laundry)	$0	$25,000
Dues and literature	$400	$400
Washer hook-up fees (sewer connection)	$22,500	$400 (new washers)
Business licenses/permits	$100	$0
Advertising/grand opening	$6,000	$500
Top-loaders ($900 each)	$27,000	$0
25-pound front-loaders ($3,000 each)	$36,000	$3,000
50-pound front-loaders ($6,000 each)	$18,000	$6,000
Stacked dryers ($4,000 each)	$64,000	$4,000 (new dryer)
Warranty on parts and service	$6,000	$2,000 (new equip.)
Card system	$30,000	$0
Software (for card system)	$8,000	$0
Water heating system	$10,000	$0
Soap dispenser	$1,500	$0
Laundry carts ($100 each)	$1,000	$0
Laundry scale	$750	$0
Cash register	$600	$0
Change machine	$0	$0
Office equipment	$250	$100
Phone installation	$60	$0
Televisions ($300 each)	$900	$300
Computers ($2,000 each)	$2,000	$0
Video security system	$0	$1,500
Miscellaneous supplies	$1,000	$400
Total Start-Up Costs	$536,060	$193,600

televisions have also been provided for the customers, at a cost of $2,900. While the owner decided to buy his own soap vending machine (for $1,500), he decided to cut costs by contracting with an outside company for soda and snack vending services. To advertise his new store, the owner took out ads in both the local newspaper and the Yellow Pages. He also organized a large grand opening to introduce his business to the neighborhood, and he sent a direct-mail advertisement with a discount coupon to potential customers in the area.

The owners of Squeaky Clean, on the other hand, bought an existing laundry located in the business district of a small town. The owners decided to renovate the 1,000-square-foot store. They wanted to repaint, replace flooring, install some better lighting, and add several new machines to meet customer demand. The renovations came to $25,000, and the new equipment cost another $13,000.

The business came with five-year-old equipment, including 10 top-loaders, three 25-pound front-loaders, five stacked dryers (i.e., ten dryers), a change machine, and a soap vending machine. The owners decided to buy and install an additional 25-pound front-loader and one 50-pound front-loader. They had to pay $200 in hook-up fees for each washer. They also had one stacked dryer (two dryers) installed to accommodate the additional volume of clothes from the front-loaders.

The owners of Squeaky Clean decided to put a television set in their store for customers to watch while waiting for their laundry. And since they did not want to hire attendants, the owners installed a video security system for safety purposes. Squeaky Clean machines take coins, and like Suds-Are-Us, the vending services are contracted. To announce that the store is under new management, the owners decided to organize a small grand opening celebration. They also placed a Yellow Pages ad.

Finding the Money

OK, you're looking at spending hundreds of thousands of dollars to buy or build a laundry. Where are you going to get all this money? Wherever you can.

"Financing is a major issue of the coin laundry industry," says CPA and laundry consultant Richard Weisinger. "Lenders want something that holds its value as collateral. Laundromat equipment is a heavily wasting asset. It wears out very quickly, and bankers are loathe to lend into an industry where the bulk of the value of the industry is tied up in intangibles [such as customer loyalty]."

That doesn't mean, however, that banks won't make loans to laundry entrepreneurs. Weisinger adds that if you have been in business before and have a good credit history, you should be able to get a loan. Most of the entrepreneurs interviewed for this book received loans from their local banks. A few also used family money. Those who had relationships with people at their banks approached them and received good deals.

Bright Idea

Consider getting a revolving line of credit from your bank, a sort of preapproved loan that lets you borrow money quickly whenever you need it. If you have a major equipment failure or fire, for example, you can get money immediately to fix the problem.

Distributors, the folks who'll sell you your equipment, will also help you finance a laundry. Many times, if a prospective owner can't get a loan from a bank, the equipment manufacturer, through the distributor, will finance a store. Paul Donovan, vice president of sales and marketing at distributor PWS, says that his company will help out an entrepreneur if he or she shows good business smarts. "What we really look for is some kind of business background," he says. "We look at their financial worth for the last three years."

He wants to see a business plan, including whether the store will be attended, what sort of services will be offered, and what kind of equipment will be promoted. "If someone comes out and says 'Here I am; I'm 26 years old, and I want to finance at 90 percent, and I've never run a business,' then we're going to be a little tougher on them," he says.

Weisinger warns that distributors often offer sandwich financing, meaning that they borrow from the bank to loan to entrepreneurs and mark up the rate. The entrepreneurs interviewed for this book said that they received a better deal from banks. "The distributor couldn't even come close," says Collette C., who runs a laundry in Evans, Colorado.

Choosing a Structure

Before you approach a lender, you should decide what sort of business structure you want to choose for your laundry. You can operate as a sole proprietor, a corporation, or a cross between them—meaning a limited liability company, an S corporation, or a partnership.

Operating as a sole proprietor is the simplest way to go—you just add a form to your personal income tax. You can use business losses to offset your personal income, thereby reducing your taxes. This is especially helpful in the first year of business, before your laundry has reached full swing. The downside is that you're personally liable in case someone falls in your laundry and sues.

At the other extreme, operating as a corporation protects your personal assets from business debts, but you can't use business losses to reduce your personal income tax. And incorporating your business is much more complicated and expensive.

The rest of the business structures you can choose from offer some sort of compromise between a sole proprietorship and a corporation.

Weisinger often recommends operating as an S corporation, but he says that a particular business structure is not crucial for laundromats. "There's no one answer," he says. "It'll depend on your exposure, the simplicity in your life. The moment you form a corporation or a limited liability company, you have just bought yourself another tax preparation fee." He also notes that while operating as a sole proprietorship makes you personally liable in case a customer sues, your insurance will pay for that.

Fun Fact

To be eligible for a loan through the Small Business Administration, you must have been turned down by two private lenders. In addition, you must be independent of larger franchises, and you must meet size requirements. See the SBA's Web site, www.sba.gov, for more information.

6

Calling in the Experts

You may have decided to start a laundry business because you like the idea of working on your own. But you can't do it all by yourself. You'll need lots of help from experts—from equipment distributors to accountants to repair technicians—to get off to a good start. In this chapter, we'll describe what these and other experts can do to help you get your laundry up and running. We'll also cover how to select good ones to work with.

Distributors

Distributors are the folks who sell you laundry equipment. Everyone who opens a new laundromat, or renovates an existing one, will need to work with a distributor before they can open their doors. Those who buy laundromats in pristine condition will eventually call on a distributor to replace worn-out washers and dryers. Distributors work regionally, and they sell equipment from certain manufacturers. So while Joe Distributor sells only Wash King brand equipment in southern Florida, for example, Jane Distributor sells only Super Suds brand equipment, and only in Montana.

These people do much more than sell equipment, however. They can advise you on almost any aspect of your laundry. Distributors will advise you first of all on your location. To determine whether the site will be successful, they will evaluate the customer base surrounding the site, as well as parking and visibility. They'll also look at whether you have enough space for the necessary equipment and whether the site can be remodeled to accommodate a laundry.

Brian D., the laundry owner in Iowa City, Iowa, already knew a distributor through his rental business. When he decided to open a laundromat, he asked the distributor about several locations he had found. The distributor nixed them all. "The guy said it wasn't going to work because of lack of parking," Brian said. Finally, he found a location his distributor did like. He built his new laundry there, and business has taken off.

Distributors will also help you with your equipment mix. They can tell you how many of each type of machine you'll need, based on the customers in your location. (We'll talk more about equipment mix in Chapter 7.) They'll also install the equipment and offer you training in maintaining and repairing it. Distributors act as brokers in buying and selling a store, too (as we mentioned in Chapter 4).

> **Bright Idea**
>
> After your laundry has been up and running for a while, ask a consultant to come and evaluate it for you to see where you could be making more money. There's bound to be something you can do to cut costs or bring in more customers.

"The distributor is really the local expert," says Brian Wallace of the Coin Laundry Association. Distributors earn their money by selling you equipment; they won't charge you for giving advice or for the time they spend explaining the business to you.

Choosing a Distributor

To find a distributor in your area, talk with other laundry owners, preferably ones that won't be in direct competition with you. Ask them whether the distributor they used was helpful, knowledgeable, and honest about potential problems. You want a distributor who will steer you away from bad locations—like the one that helped Brian D. in Iowa City.

Also contact your local coin laundry association. These organizations have collective knowledge about distributors in your area and should be able to refer you to someone. Take the time to interview any distributors who have been recommended to you. You'll be working with your distributor very closely for a while, so you want to find someone with whom you feel comfortable. Make sure he or she is responsive to questions, personable, and easy to talk with.

"I highly recommend that people who get into the business interview multiple distributors," says Wallace. Although each distributor sells only one or maybe two makes of equipment, Wallace and other experts recommend that new laundry owners choose a person rather than a machine. The various brands of washers and dryers being manufactured now are all top quality, they say. What will really cause a difference in your business is a good distributor who can advise you well.

"It's really more important who you buy from than what you buy," Wallace says. "You'd much rather find a distributor who's knowledgeable of the industry, or that particular market, and use whatever brand of equipment they happen to carry."

"I agree completely," says Paul Partyka of *American Coin-Op* magazine. "Go with the distributor rather than the equipment." He says that a few people have preferences for certain brands but adds that all brands seem to perform well. "I think people are generally satisfied with their equipment."

A Second Opinion

Wise distributors know that they will do well in the long run if they advise you honestly and help you avoid pitfalls. If your store is successful, you'll likely want to open another one. Or you will recommend them to new owners.

But not all distributors are wise. And keep in mind that your distributor is in the business to sell you equipment. Distributors don't make any money unless you buy or build a store. "[Distributors] are the worst possible people to go to to get an unbiased opinion," says Richard Weisinger, a laundry consultant.

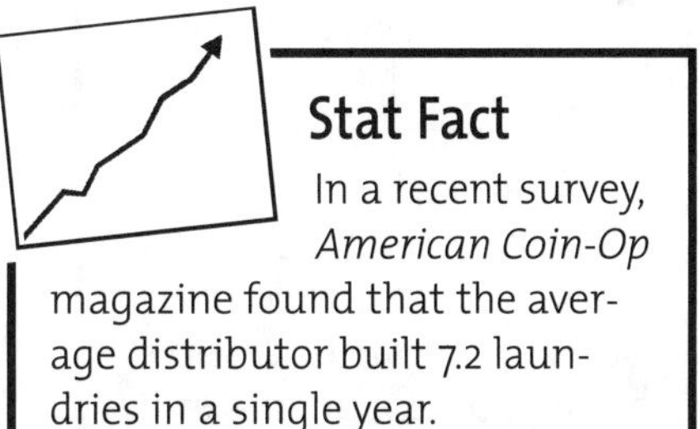

Stat Fact
In a recent survey, *American Coin-Op* magazine found that the average distributor built 7.2 laundries in a single year.

"That has nothing to do with their integrity or lack of it. It is simply how they earn their living—by selling stores."

When you're buying a laundry, or building a new one, you're paying hundreds of thousands of dollars, so it's smart to play it safe. Get a second opinion. Even if you'd trust your distributor with your kids on a white-water rafting trip in the middle of winter, it's still a good idea to get someone else's viewpoint. The second opinion could come from another distributor, experienced laundry owners, your laundry association, or a consultant.

Consultants

There's a small group of people, most of them former laundry owners, who act as consultants for the laundry industry. You pay them by the hour, so they have no interest in whether you buy equipment or a particular store, or whether you even get into the laundry business.

Consultants will tell you if they think your location is good, whether your equipment mix is correct, whether the rent is fair, and what sort of profit you can expect from a certain store. They may even be able to estimate how many turns a day you can expect (how many times each piece of equipment will be used each day). This estimate will help you to price your services correctly.

They can inspect a store and tell you what sort of shape the equipment is in; they can also tell you if there are any problems with the building itself. Consultants can advise you on how to run a wash-and-fold service and how to supervise your employees. Most importantly, they can determine how much a store is worth. In short, a consultant can advise you on just about every aspect of your business. They will cost you, though. Consultants charge from $100 to $200 an hour. For a listing of several laundry consultants, take a look at the Appendix in the back of the book.

Contractors

If you are building a new laundry, or renovating an existing one, you'll need to hire a contractor (unless you are a contractor, like Dave A., one of our entrepreneurs). There are a few contractors who specialize in laundries, but don't go too much out of your way to find one. Plumbing is plumbing, and tiling is tiling—whether it's for a house or for a laundromat.

"There really isn't that much difference between the construction of a laundry and any other kind of construction," says laundry consultant

Beware!

Make sure any contractor you hire is bonded. This means the contractor is insured, so you won't be liable in case of injury or accidents on the job. It also protects you in case the contractor destroys any equipment or creates any structural damage.

Lionel Bogut. "It's not that different from what it is in an average home. Just find an experienced, all-around good contractor."

The best way to find a good contractor is to ask everyone you know—neighbors, business associates, and friends—for recommendations. Contact those who are recommended to you and ask them to give you an estimate of how much it will cost to build or renovate your laundry. Don't just go with the cheapest one—you don't want anyone to cut corners. Try to find a happy medium between price and quality. And before you hire your contractor, be sure to verify that he is properly licensed.

Dollar Stretcher

If you want to use a consultant, gather beforehand all the information about the laundry you want to purchase—demographics, a copy of the lease, information on fees and permits, utility bills, expense and income reports from the current owner, a pro forma from a distributor, and warranties. That way, you save yourself the hourly cost of having the consultant do this preliminary research.

Designers

You may also want to work with a designer or architect when building or renovating your laundry. Most of the entrepreneurs interviewed for this book just designed their stores with the help of their distributors, but a few did choose to hire a professional designer.

Brian D., who wanted a bold image for his store, gathered photographs of laundromats he liked and took them to a designer. The two of them worked together to create a store that made them both happy. With its bright colors and bold signs, Brian says, his store has the kind of look he wants—fresh and new.

Repair Technicians

Unless you're very handy and expect to fix the machines in your store by yourself, you will likely need a repair technician. Don't wait until a machine breaks to find one, though. It's much better to have a repair technician lined up beforehand. If you have a regular repair technician, you can get your machines fixed quickly and efficiently by someone you know is competent.

Janet H., who owns a laundry in Fullerton, California, has a repair technician on a retainer. She pays him to come in once a week and check all the machines. If she knows that certain machines need repair, she notes that on a clipboard that she leaves for him. Janet pays for parts and keeps a small inventory at the laundry so the repair technician can fix machines quickly. If her repair technician needs to spend much more time than usual repairing her machines, Janet pays him extra.

Another option is to use the repair service offered by your equipment manufacturer; ask your distributor about going this route. You can also check with other laundry owners in your area to find out if they know of an independent repair technician. You can expect to pay repair technician between $100 and $300 a week, depending on the size of your laundry.

Other Expertise

When you're setting up your business, you should also hire the services of an attorney or an accountant. These professionals will help you decide on an appropriate business structure and make sure you're up on all the tax issues. As with hiring a repair technician, it's best to find a good lawyer or accountant before a crisis situation. How do you choose a good one? Rather than just flipping through the Yellow Pages, you should contact your local bar association for a referral. Another option is to ask other professionals you know, such as bankers or business owners in the laundry industry. You can network with other laundry owners through your local coin laundry association and ask for their recommendations.

It's best to find a good lawyer or accountant before a crisis situation.

Association Expertise

Professional associations can provide invaluable help to new business owners. The staff and members are usually very experienced and knowledgeable about their industry, and they're eager to provide an unbiased opinion (as long as you're a member).

There is only one national laundry association, the Coin Laundry Association (it covers card-operated laundries, too); it has several affiliate organizations around the country. There are also separate regional associations—ask laundry owners in your area where you can find these groups.

Associations hold meetings and other networking opportunities and often publish guidebooks and newsletters, which they issue at a discount for members. Annual dues for associations usually run from $150 to $250. The Coin Laundry Association has a hotline for its members. If you're unsure about any aspect of your business—whether it's location, the right equipment mix, or anything else—you can call during business hours and ask the opinion of an expert.

7

Getting Equipped

A laundromat is all about the equipment inside it. While good customer service will help attract repeat business to your store, having the right number of quality machines (all in good working order) is paramount to your success. This chapter will cover the basic laundry equipment you'll need for your store: washers, dryers, water heaters, change

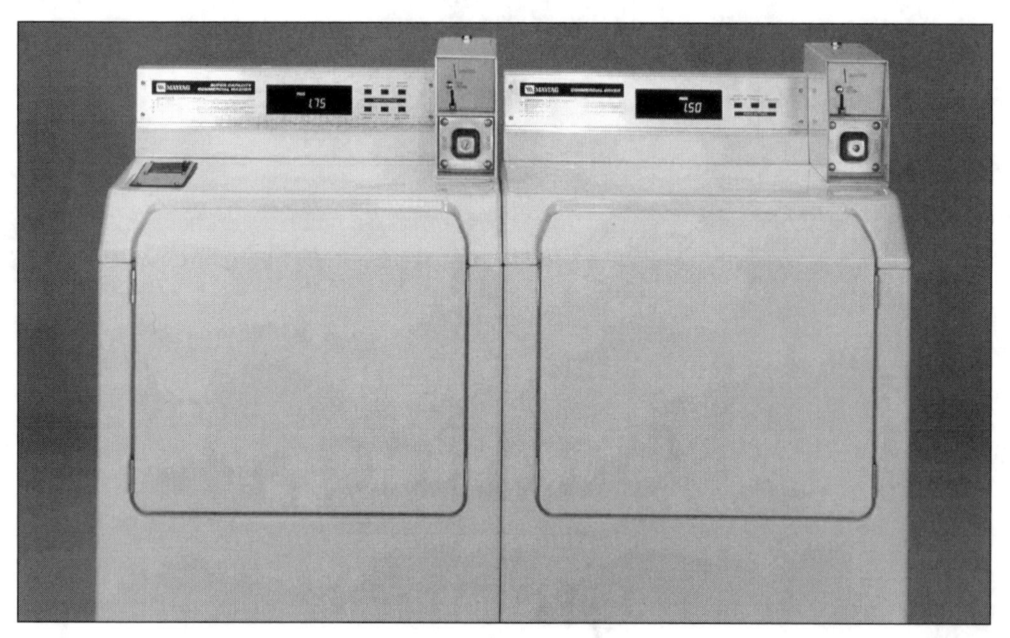

Photo Courtesy: Maytag

machines, folding tables, and laundry carts. We'll talk about the ideal equipment mix for your laundry and how to arrange equipment inside your store. We'll also look at the "Coin vs. Card" debate and find out why one system may be better than the other for your laundromat.

Machine Basics

Customers will visit a laundromat to use three types of machines: top-load washers, front-load washers, and dryers. The top-loaders are the standard washing machines you find in homes—with a door that opens on top and an agitator in the middle. These can hold about eight pounds of laundry.

Front-loaders are large washing machines with a door in the front and a drum that looks like those in a dryer. These come in various sizes, and people in the industry refer to them according to how much laundry the machines can hold, such as 25-pound front-loaders or 35-pounders. The smallest of these washers can hold 18 pounds of laundry, the largest as much as 80 pounds. Front-loaders use about half as

Dollar Stretcher

Purchase parts for your machines and supplies, such as toilet paper and cleaning fluids, in bulk. You'll not only get a discount, but you'll save on the time spent buying these goods.

much water as top-loaders per pound of wash: An 18-pound front-loader, for example, will use the same amount of water as a top-loader. These machines are real moneymakers for laundry businesses because they're so efficient.

The dryers in laundromats are similar to dryers in homes, except that they are larger. They can hold two loads of laundry from a top-load washer. Most commercial dryers manufactured these days are stacked dryers, which means two dryers sit one on top of the other in a joined cabinet casing. If you have 20 stacked dryers in your store, you have a total of 40 dryers for customers to use.

The Right Mix

When you're setting up your laundry, you should think about what types of machines you want to install and how many of each you will need. The first thing to consider is whether you'll have the right ratio of washers to dryers. If you have too few dryers, for example, your customers will have to wait around before they can take their clothes out of the washer and put them in the dryer. This means that other customers won't be able to get their laundry started and may go to another laundry instead.

The rule of thumb in the industry is to have one dryer for every two top-load washers and one for each front-load washer. This rule is based on the fact that customers generally put two loads of laundry from top-load washing machines into one dryer. If they use the front-loaders, however, they generally place one load of laundry into one dryer. Since drying can take a little longer than washing, some experts recommend that you add a few extra dryers above this estimate. "If you have 40 top-loaders, you want 21 to 22 dryers," says consultant Lionel Bogut. With the right equipment mix, he says, your customers can flow through your laundry quickly,

Speedy Spinner

Besides washers and dryers, there's one more type of machine your customers can use: extractors. These are machines that spin at high speeds and take out much of the water left after the washer spin cycle. They can reduce drying time by as much as half.

Craig H. has an extractor in one of his laundries in Washington state. He said his customers like to use it for items that absorb a lot of water such as towels and bedspreads because it cuts down on the drying time. "It's good for comforters and other items that can't take a lot of heat," he says. The extractor costs customers $.69 a load to use.

leaving room for the next customer. "You have to constantly look at turnover in the laundry. In many laundries you can increase business by taking out machines and putting in folding areas and dryers."

Next, you'll need to consider the number of top-loaders as compared to the number of front-loaders. This is trickier since it depends on your location. Customers who wash large loads every week are more likely to use the front-loaders because these machines usually offer them a better deal. A front-loader can wash more than twice the amount of laundry that a top-load washer can—for less than twice the price. Customers also use front-loaders to wash large items such as quilts and sleeping bags. So a laundromat in a neighborhood with lots of families is going to need many front-loaders.

A laundry near a college or senior residence, on the other hand, will need more top-loaders. Most of these people will be single and won't have enough clothes every week to justify the large machines. "People who have only one load of whites, one load of mediums, [and] one load of darks aren't going to use the front-loaders," says Janet H., who owns a laundry in Fullerton, California. To determine the right mix, she says, you need to find out how many apartments and single-family homes there are in the area, as well as the income levels of your potential customers.

It's always a good idea to discuss equipment mix with your distributor, too. With his or her expertise, you should be able to determine the sort of mix that will suit your store best.

Where Everything Goes

If it's possible in your space, you want to place your washers and dryers opposite each other. For example, if your laundry is long and narrow, you want to put all the washers on one side and all the dryers on the other. Or if you have an island of machines intersecting the store, you could put all the washers against the walls and the dryers in the middle. This set-up lets customers move their laundry quickly from one machine to the next, and it makes room for the next customer. See the "Floor Plan" on page 71.

Machines that are placed opposite each other should be spaced at least four feet apart, though six feet is better, says laundry consultant Tim Craig. "There has to be enough space so that the customers are not bumping into each other," he says.

Tip...

Smart Tip

To help customers get their clothes from the washers to the dryers, you should provide them with laundry carts they can wheel around. Owners of unattended laundries complain that these tend to disappear; however, you can buy carts with vertical bars that prevent customers from taking them out the door.

Although some of your customers are going to shove their clothes right from the dryer into their duffel bags and set off for home, most of them are going to be a little neater with their clothing. You'll need folding tables—counter-high tables—that customers can use to put their clothes, sheets, or towels in order before they take them home. Place the folding tables near the dryers so customers can dump their laundry directly from the dryers onto the tables. If you have folding tables placed opposite washers or dryers, allow at least four feet between the tables and the machines; you

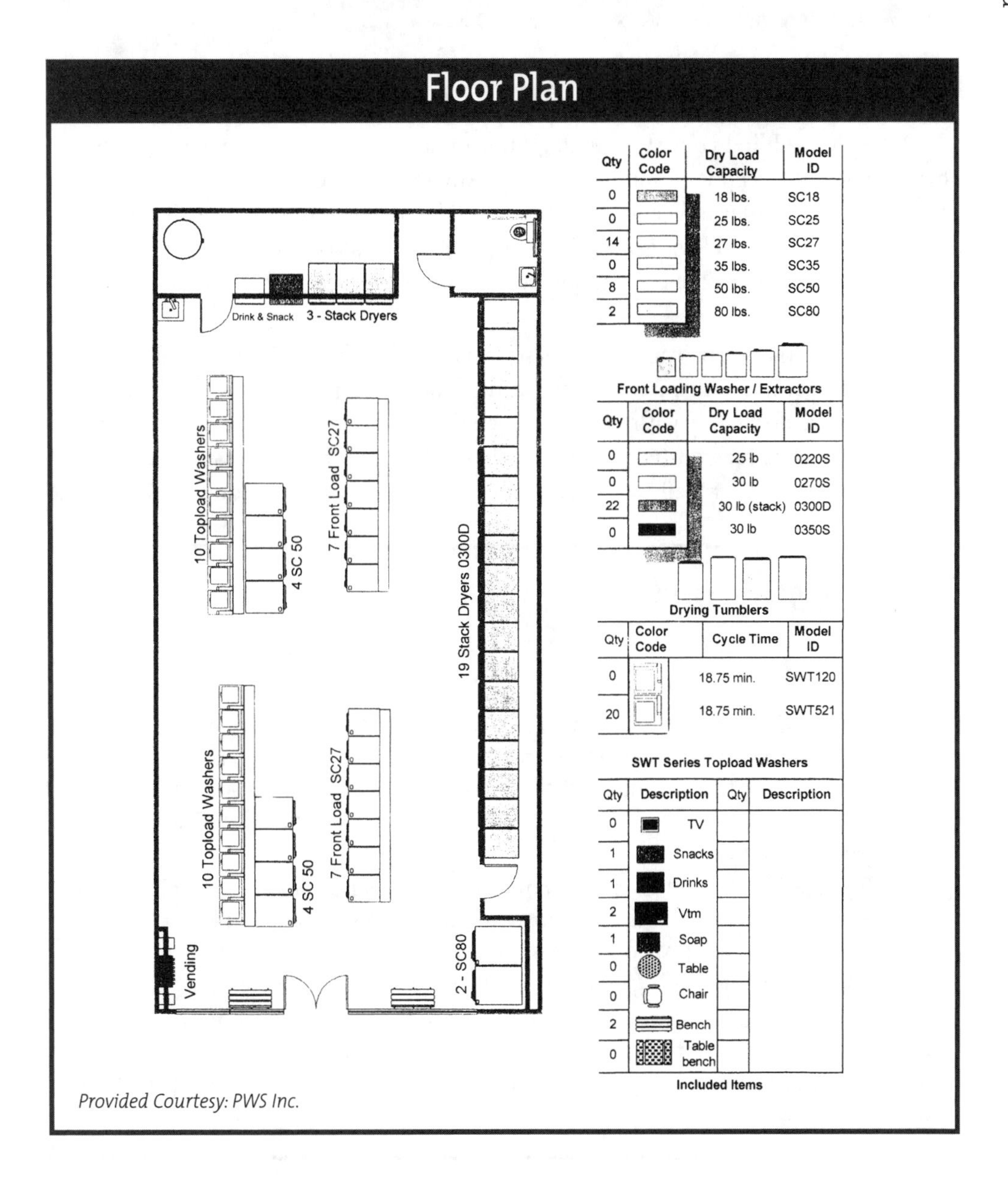

Provided Courtesy: PWS Inc.

want your customers to have adequate space to transfer their laundry between the machines and from the dryers to the counters.

It's best to place your front-load washers as close to the entrance of the store as possible. Customers who come in with huge bags of laundry will want to unload them as soon as possible. Another reason for this placement is that customers are more likely to use front-loaders if those are the washing machines they see first. Remember: It's to your advantage to have customers use front-load washers, because these machines bring in more money than top-loaders while using less water for each pound of laundry.

Equipment TLC

Once you've filled your store with all this great equipment, you need to do everything you can to keep it running smoothly. Any store can expect to have one or two machines out of order now and then, but you'll be losing a lot of money if more than that are on the fritz. Having machines in poor repair also sends a message to your customers that you don't care about your store—a message that won't encourage repeat business.

So you'll want to repair machines as soon as they break. In addition, you may want to consider preventive maintenance to head off potential problems with older equipment. If you're not handy with machines, don't panic. You can hire a repair technician to do all the work for you (take a look back at Chapter 6 for a refresher). But if you can do some of the repair work yourself, you'll save money. You'll also get the

Not Just Quarters

Laundry owner Robert G., who bought a laundromat that ran on quarters, started having problems with noncustomers using his change machine. "They were taking the change for the bus and the parking meters, and leaving my customers with no change," he says. Rather than install a card system, he decided to go with dollar coins.

"I figured 'I'll get them,' and I switched over to the Susan B. Anthony dollars." He had to alter his washers himself because manufacturers didn't build the right kind of slide. The dryers still run on quarters. He also had to retrofit his change machine, which now gives three of the dollar coins and eight quarters for each $5 bill.

At first, he said, his customers would confuse the Susan B. Anthony coins with quarters, but they eventually realized they were dollars. Now he uses the golden Sacagawea coin, which his customers like better because you can't confuse these dollar coins with quarters.

machines up and running more quickly if you jump on the problem rather than wait for the repair technician to show up. Most of the entrepreneurs interviewed for this book knew next to nothing about laundry equipment when they started their businesses, yet they are doing many of the necessary repairs themselves.

"We're learning by trial and error," says Collette C. in Evans, Colorado. She and her partner, Kim C., attended a repair school offered by their distributor. They found it very helpful, she says, and would recommend it to new laundry owners.

In Hot Water

That little water heater in your home that runs out of hot water after three showers isn't going to cut it for your laundromat. You'll need a sophisticated water heating system that will provide enough hot water for everyone, quickly. Some systems circulate water continuously throughout the store so that even the washers furthest from the heater provide hot water as soon as customers need it.

You might also want to think about a heat recovery system for hot water. These new systems save energy and cut utility bills—one of your biggest expenses. They work by running cold incoming water through coils that wrap around the waste water pipe. When hot water drains through the pipe, the water in the coils gets heated. This fresh, warm water then goes to the water heater where it will be heated up the rest of the way. Since less energy is needed to heat the warmed water, you will save on your monthly gas bill.

Determining which system is the best for your store will depend on the size of your laundry, the hours it's open, the price of utilities, and other factors. Talk with your distributor and your contractor about choosing the right water heating system for your store.

The Card Advantage

As we have mentioned briefly already, manufacturers now build washers and dryers that take cards rather than coins. Card systems are a fairly recent development, though. Brian Wallace of the Coin Laundry Association estimates that only 400 to 500 of the 30,000 or so laundries in the country are card operated.

In a laundry with a card system, customers purchase a card from a card machine, often making a deposit of a few dollars for the card. The rest of the money is stored on the card much like it is on a phone card. Customers then swipe the card through the machines they want to use, and the machines subtract the price. If a customer puts too much money on a card, you can refund the amount left on the card.

There are many advantages to having a card system in your laundry:

- *With a card system, you can change prices at any time.* You can raise prices by pennies rather than 25 cents.
- *You can also issue discount cards that take off less money with each swipe.* You can offer a discount to your regular customers by giving $22 of equipment use for $20, for example. You can easily offer specials to students or seniors or to customers who use the laundry during slow periods.

> Tip...
>
> **Smart Tip**
>
> Your customer base may determine whether a card system will work for your store. Seniors are often more apprehensive about using cards, and tourists often don't want the trouble of buying a card and figuring out the system for just one or two visits.

- *You don't have to carry around bags of coins.* This also means you don't have to count coins.
- *You get paid in advance.* A customer will put $20 or $30 on a card, then hold on to it until the following week.
- *The card keeps customers coming back to your store.* Since customers often add more value to their card than they intend to use in one trip, you know they'll be returning to use up the balance.
- *A card system includes a software program.* This program will automatically compute for you which machines are being used and how often—that means less work for you.

"It is far and away better than coins," says Janet H. "I did 20 years of coins, and you couldn't get me to do that again." She says she doesn't miss pulling money from the machines, lugging bags of coins, counting them, and depositing them in the bank.

Janet also likes the software that comes with the system. The software records each time a machine is used. It can even tell what type of card (senior- or student-discount card, or attendant's card) was used. Janet says there's an added benefit: Since she knows which machines are getting used more often, she can switch them around periodically so they wear at the same rate.

Craig H., who owns three card-operated laundries in Washington state, agrees that the card system offers a great management tool. "It provides us with a better picture of how the laundry is working and how to manage it better. We know which size dryer is working and what time of day." He also says that he offers his customers an incentive to use cards—an extra dollar added to the value of their card for every $10 they put in the card machine. You may want to offer a bonus like this, though customers may prefer the card system even without it. Craig says, "The customers like [cards] because you don't have to fool around with quarters—'ca-chunk, ca-chunk, ca-chunk'—[to] drop them in the slots."

Paul Donovan, with PWS distributors in Los Angeles, says that all the stores his company is building now are card stores. However, converting an old store to the card system is expensive and probably not cost-effective, he says.

Keep the following guidelines in mind when making a decision between a card system and the traditional coin system. A card system may be the best choice for your store if:

- You have the money to purchase the system.
- Your customers tend to be regulars.
- You want to give discounts and specials to certain groups.
- You don't want to carry around bags of coins.
- Noncustomers keep using your change machines for bus or parking fares.

Beware!

To discourage counterfeiters, the U.S. mint issues new bills and coins every few years. Older coin changers may not be able to read the new bills. When you're purchasing a changer (or a store with a changer), make sure it can accept the newest bills from the mint. Some changers also come with low-cost or free upgrades.

Happy with Coins

Not everyone is sold on card systems. Several of the entrepreneurs interviewed for this book decided against cards when they built their stores. They didn't want to pay the extra $20,000 to $30,000 for the system, and they felt customers would be more comfortable with coins.

Collette C. says she and her partner considered cards but decided against them after talking with other laundry owners. "With quarters, it's something people always have," she says. "They don't like having to buy the card. They like having the freedom to come and go as they please, and go where they want."

Dave A., who owns a laundry in New Glarus, Wisconsin, also decided not to use the card system. Dave built his laundry next to a coin-operated car wash, so he figured customers from the car wash would be more likely to use his laundry if it were coin-operated as well. Another consideration for Dave was the fact that New Glarus is a tourist town, so much of his business consists of one-time-only customers. He felt that customers wouldn't want to go to the trouble of buying a card. Even if they did, he has an unattended laundry and wouldn't be able to give refunds to anyone with value left on a card at the end of their vacation. "[My distributor] felt with the tourist trade that it made more sense." Dave says it was the right decision: "I've never heard anyone complain about our coin system."

Tip...

Smart Tip

If you have an unattended laundry, always have two working coin changers. If one machine breaks or runs out of coins, customers can use the other one, and you'll keep them in your store.

If you go with coins over cards, you must have change machines in your store. Change machines are the lifeblood of any coin-operated laundry. If customers can't make change, they can't use your machines, and you'll be out of business in a hurry. You may want to have two, just in case one breaks. Place both near the front window to discourage theft and always be sure they're in good working condition.

As you weigh the pros and cons of going with a coin system, see if the factors listed below apply to you. Coins may be a better choice for your laundry if:

- You don't want to pay for an expensive card system.
- Many of your customers are vacationers or infrequent users who are not likely to buy cards.
- Your customers speak different languages, and you won't be able to explain the system to everyone.
- You don't have an attendant to help customers use the system and give customers refunds.

8

Dressing the Store

If you're building a laundromat, you'll need to do more to your store than just load it with equipment—you'll need to design and decorate it. If you're buying an existing laundromat, you'll likely want to update its appearance. A well-decorated store isn't just pleasing to the eye. As we've said before, the laundry industry is a mature industry, so you'll need to use everything in your arsenal to win customers from your competitors.

You'll want to start with a store that looks good and feels comfortable; after all, you need to provide customers with a more pleasant atmosphere than what your competition offers. A little entertainment, for adults and children alike, goes a long way toward winning customers. A laundry chain in Southern California, for example, includes a sandwich shop and a coffee bar. Customers can dump a load of clothes, then go have a snack or a cup of Joe while they're waiting. Others have tanning salons, cafés, or even mailboxes for rent. This chapter will cover decorating and amenities—the fine touches that will keep your customers returning.

General Guidelines

When it comes to putting in the major components of your store's interior—flooring, windows, lighting, and signs—first of all, think clean. We're back to that familiar refrain: Customers want to visit a clean store. They'll be visiting your laundry to get clothes clean, not to dirty them in dryers that have mysterious substances stuck inside or on folding tables that haven't been wiped down. Anything you can do to enhance the cleanliness of your store will reassure customers.

Besides, it's much more pleasant to hang around in a nice-looking store—your customers have to stay there a couple of hours, so give them something enjoyable to see. They don't want to stay in a store with peeling paint, burned-out light bulbs, and cracked ceiling tiles. By keeping your store looking nice, you give customers the message that you care about them and want their business.

Here are some general pointers for decorating your laundry:

- *Go for a modern appearance.* If your store looks like it hasn't been touched since 1965, customers will wonder not only about its cleanliness but whether the equipment works.
- *Use lighter colors for walls, ceilings, and floors.* These areas reflect light; as a result, your store will appear brighter if you use lighter colors. With reflected light, you may also spend less on electricity.
- *Keep the design of the store as open as possible.* You don't want any hidden spaces where thieves can lurk.
- *Use adequate lighting.* Customers want to see their clothes clearly, and they want to feel safe.

Floor It

Choosing flooring for your store will be one of your most important decorating decisions. The first thing customers will notice is the floor, so you want to make a strong statement. Collette C., who runs a laundry with her partner in Evans, Colorado,

> **Bright Idea**
> Place your coin changers near the front window of your laundromat so people on the street can see them. Also make sure they're well lit. Thieves are less likely to try to break into change machines when they have an audience.

says they chose white floor tiles for their store because white looked cleaner than any other color.

Since you or your employees will be mopping the floor every day, you want your flooring to be easy to clean, too. Tiles and certain types of linoleum are best; carpeting is not. Dave A., who owns a laundry in New Glarus, Wisconsin, chose carpeting for his store, a decision he now regrets. While carpeting is comfortable for his customers to stand on, he and his wife find it too difficult to clean. They have to vacuum it daily and shampoo it frequently. "We'll be replacing it with tile pretty soon," he says.

Keep in mind that you want a floor that's skidproof. If a washer leaks or a customer spills some water, you don't want all your employees and customers sliding and crashing onto the floor.

Finally, you want a floor that will be as resistant as possible to water damage. Check with your contractor about good quality flooring that offers durability, traction, and a surface that's easy to clean.

Window Dressing

Be sure to front your store with large, plate-glass windows. Windows showcase your laundromat, which may attract customers who decide they like the look of your store. They also give customers a sense of security, since passersby can easily see what's happening inside the store. And large windows let you capture natural light, saving electricity and providing a more comfortable atmosphere.

Sign Away

You'll need signs inside your laundry, both to inform customers about your policies and to protect yourself against liability. Don't handwrite your signs: Spend the money to have some printed. This tells your customers that you're a professional laundry owner who cares about your store's appearance.

When coming up with the text for your signs, avoid the "No" syndrome—as in "No Smoking," "No Sitting on Equipment," "No Loitering," "No Eating," etc. No one likes being lectured,

> **Beware!**
> Don't place too many signs in your windows. For safety reasons, you want to keep those panes of glass as open as possible.

so at least try to use the word "please." You'll find customers more willing to follow your rules if you speak to them nicely. Also try to give them alternatives: For example, "Please don't smoke inside. We have a bench outside for those of you who smoke."

Be sure to place signs saying that you are not responsible for theft or damage. This will help you in case of lawsuits. Finally, put up signs in all the languages your customers speak. If your laundry is in a neighborhood populated with Vietnamese immigrants, for example, get help from someone who speaks the language, or hire a translator to write signs in Vietnamese. Those potential customers who don't speak English will feel welcome at your store.

Setting Yourself Apart

Consider giving your store a theme or a gimmick. For example, one store in San Francisco plays classic black-and-white movies on their television, and the walls are covered with photographs of movie stars from the 1920s and 1930s. Another store in Texas displays the owner's collection of antique laundry equipment. Iowa City laundry owner Brian D. chose humor: He plays comedy channels on his televisions and places signs with clever puns, such as "We have a dryer sense of humor" and "We never clothes." (His store is open 24 hours a day.)

A theme gives your store more personality; customers will remember it, and they'll find your laundry a more interesting place to visit. A clever gimmick may also get you some free publicity from the local press. If you want to create a gimmick for your laundromat, think about who your customers are and what sort of theme they will appreciate. One owner in Southern California, whose customers hail from all over

From Palm Trees to Planets

If you choose to incorporate a theme in the décor of your laundry, here are some ideas to get you started:

- *The Old West.* You could have cowboy music on the radio, westerns on the TV, Texas landscapes on the walls, and a rocking horse for the children.
- *The Tropics.* Your store could be transformed with palm trees (real or fake), Hawaiian shirts on the walls, and surf tunes on the radio.
- *Outer Space.* You could run science fiction movies on the TV, have a rocket model that kids can play on, and paint the walls with stars and planets.

Latin America, hung his laundry with flags from several of his customers' native homelands and started serving traditional Latin American food.

Beware!

Don't forget to look at your laundromat from a toddler's point of view. Get down on your hands and knees, and crawl all around your store looking for potential hazards. You'll likely see some things you've never noticed before that might be relatively easy to fix.

For the Little Kids

Many laundry owners are realizing that they can increase business by providing a play area for children. Often, customers need to bring their children to the laundromat, so giving little ones something to do makes the laundry chore much easier on parents. Having an area set aside for children can also help keep them from running around and possibly getting hurt or damaging equipment.

Janet H., who owns a laundry in Fullerton, California, has a separate room with a large window for the children. The room has little chairs and a TV with a video player that sits in the attendants' area. Janet has a collection of about 60 children's videos, and she adds to it every month or so. The children can request a video, and the attendants play it for them.

Janet says having a room dedicated to children is so helpful to parents that they choose her laundry over others. Although the room takes up space that could hold more equipment, she says, "it's paying for itself in the business I do as a result of it. I would never do away with that room."

Collette C. and her partner also have a play area for children. They have a TV with a VCR, children's videos, and toys. "We wind up picking up a lot of toys," she says, "but they love it."

If you want to put in an area specifically for children, check with your insurance agent and your city or county officials regarding liability issues. These professionals should be able to tell you how to design the area to maximize safety and make sure you won't be responsible in case a child gets hurt. In fact, you may need to place signs saying you're not responsible for children's safety.

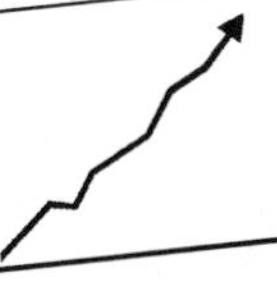

Stat Fact

According to a recent survey by Ulrich Research Services, 42 percent of people said they like to watch television while they fold laundry—the most popular activity to undertake while cleaning clothes.

For the Big Kids

Even adults will get bored at a laundromat. After all, mostly what they are doing is waiting around for clothes to wash and dry. Many laundries these days have one or more televisions mounted to the wall. Some laundries keep the televisions tuned to one channel, some play videos, and others let customers change the channels themselves.

If your laundry is unattended and you want to let customers change the channel, mount the TV low enough on the wall so they can reach the channel and volume buttons. Customers are likely to walk off with a remote control, even if it's tacked to a table.

Some laundries are also putting in computers. Collette C. has two computers in her laundry with modems so customers can surf the Internet. "They're always in use," she says.

Brian D. doesn't have computers, but he put in phone jacks near a table so customers can plug in their laptops. He placed a sign above the table saying "Internet Access," to let customers know about the service. "People have expressed that they really appreciate it," he says. To ensure people don't walk in with a phone and call Finland or Saudi Arabia, Brian has put toll restrictions on the lines.

Many laundry owners also have pinball and video games for their customers. If you want to offer your customers these games, you can contract with a vending service that

To Smoke or Not to Smoke

The smoking decision may not be up to you. Some cities and states are passing laws banning smoking in all public areas, including laundromats. But if you do have a choice, here are a few things to consider.

Laundry owners who have decided to ban smoking in their stores say their customers (even the smokers) appreciate cleaner-smelling clothing. And the nonsmokers like the cleaner air. Other laundry owners say their smoking customers don't like having to stand outside, especially in foul weather, or having to wait until their wash is done to light up.

If you decide to ban smoking, place signs around your store reminding customers not to smoke. Try making humorous ones, such as "You light up my day—just don't light up in the laundry. Please refrain from smoking." Jokes help soften the blow to those customers dying for a nicotine fix. You or your attendants may have to remind smokers for the first few months after you open or after you decide to go smoke-free.

And if you are going to ask customers to smoke outside, be sure to place a container for cigarette butts, such as an umbrella stand filled with sand, outside the door. Chairs or benches let smokers relax while they're waiting for laundry and enjoying a smoke. And a sign saying "Smoking Area" lets smokers know that they're still welcome at your laundry.

owns the machines and services them—splitting the profits with you. It won't cost you anything to put them in your store. You can talk to your distributor to find vendors that specialize in game machines.

Snack Time

It's likely that your customers will get hungry and thirsty while they're waiting for their laundry to finish. Even if your store is near a shopping area, many customers wisely don't want to leave their clothes. So vending machines with sodas, chips, and candy fit the bill. You can buy a vending machine, fill it yourself and take all the profits. Or you can contract with a vendor who will provide the machine and snacks, and split the profits with you. Ask your distributor about vending companies in your area.

Collette C. and her partner, Kim C., decided to put in a snack counter rather than vending machines. They sell their customers—and anyone else who comes in—a soda in a glass with ice, along with candy bars and chips. The partners chose to go that route after talking with other laundry owners. "In interviewing other people, we found that [they] didn't like cans, they liked a fountain drink," Collette says.

They sell the snacks at a low cost because their store is next to a minimart. "If we had the same prices or higher, everyone would just go next door," Collette says. Still, their snack business is brisk enough that it brings in $30 to $60 a day. "Our Pepsi distributor says we do more [business] than some of his restaurants." Having the snack counter also improves customer relations, Collette says. "Our customers really appreciate the cheap prices."

9

The Attended Laundry

As mentioned in the previous chapter, many laundries offer their customers a variety of services to make their in-store experience more enjoyable. But besides offering amenities such as snacks or computers, there are other important services to consider for your start-up. If you plan to have an attended laundry, you should definitely consider offering laundry-related

Photo Courtesy: The Last Load

services including wash-and-fold, and an area to drop off and pick up dry cleaning. In this chapter, we'll explore how to incorporate these services into your store and profit from them.

We'll also look at what's involved in taking on employees to attend your store. We'll discuss some of the pros and cons of hiring attendants; then we'll get into the details of hiring, supervising, and motivating employees.

Wash-and-Fold

If you're interested in starting a wash-and-fold service (also called *drop-off* or *fluff-and-fold*), take a look at the neighborhood surrounding your laundromat. Customers who use wash-and-fold are usually middle- to upper-income types who may or may not have laundry equipment at home. They use the service primarily to save time. So if your laundry is located in an area that has residents with a range of income levels, wash-and-fold could be a good complement to your coin- or card-operated laundry business.

According to laundry consultant Tim Craig, wash-and-fold produces a tidy profit for some stores and not for others. "In some places that goes really well, and in other places they can't seem to get it off the ground," he says. Craig adds that it's often difficult to determine whether a wash-and-fold service is going to take off.

As long as you plan to have an attended laundry, though, there's little reason not to give wash-and-fold a try. Starting a wash-and-fold service will cost you little—possibly less than $500. Even if the service never quite becomes a hit, it can still bring in some money at very little cost. You'll be paying your attendants the same amount whether they do wash-and-fold or not. In fact, many laundry owners offer their customers wash-and-fold service to help cover attendants' salaries.

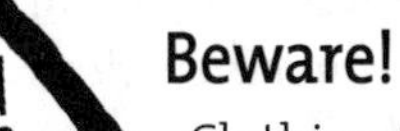

Beware!

Clothing that is stained with grease, oil, or some other flammable substance could cause a dryer fire. Make sure anything you or your attendants wash is fully cleaned before it goes into a dryer. Also, watch for customers who throw clothing in the dryer without running it through the wash first.

Janet H. decided to offer wash-and-fold when she rebuilt her laundromat after a fire. "I wanted to have an attended store, so there was approximately $3,500 of expense each month that I added that I didn't have before," says Janet, who runs a store in Fullerton, California. How could she afford to pay for this? Her wash-and-fold service has been very successful, and Janet has found that it more than pays her attendants' salaries.

How It Works

The equipment you'll need for a wash-and-fold service is minimal: a scale, a book of invoices, plastic laundry bags, stain removers, and detergent. You can buy a scale and the plastic bags from your distributor or a laundry supply company. You can purchase generic invoices from an office supply store, or you can have some printed up with your store's name and policies on them (see the sample invoice on page 89).

Once you start your wash-and-fold service, put up a sign in your laundry to let customers know you're offering this new service. Since they might not understand what "wash-and-fold" means, put up a sign that says something like, "We'll do your laundry for you." Also provide a counter so customers know where to bring their laundry. It helps to have a sign saying, "Drop your laundry here." In a large laundromat full of washers and dryers, folding tables, and vending machines, it's not always clear to customers where they should bring their clothes.

To provide basic wash-and-fold service, you or your attendant should follow these steps:

- *When a customer brings in laundry for wash-and-fold, weigh it in front of them so they know how much it will cost.* Write the weight down on the invoice, along with the total cost. Make sure you get your customers' names and phone numbers in case they forget to pick up their clothes. Tell them when their clothes will be ready and give them their copy of the invoice.

Janet H. has her attendants write down any important notes on the invoice, like whether laundry is brought in damp or wet (customers sometimes bring in towels wet from the shower or swimming). She does this in case customers complain that some of their clothes are missing if their laundry weighs less when they pick it up than it did when they dropped it off.

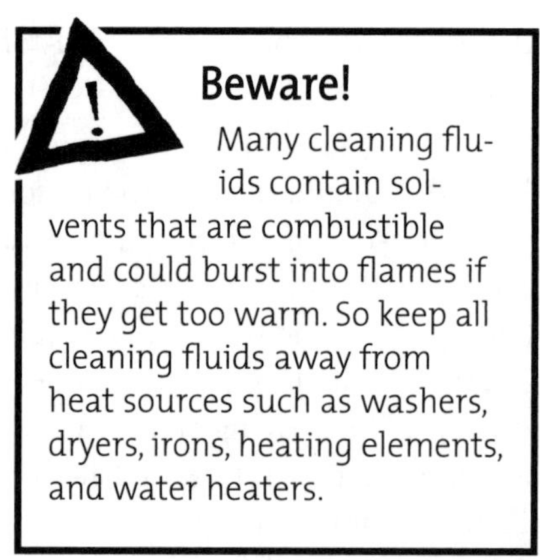

- *Check the clothes for any stains and pretreat them as well as you can.* There are several good books available for treating stains—see the Appendix for more information. These books can tell you what stain-removing products you'll need to buy and which of these to use on different types of stains.

  Collette C., with the laundry in Evans, Colorado, says she and her attendants do their best to remove all the stains on the clothes. "We don't charge extra," she says. But they also don't promise they'll be able to remove them. Check to make sure there's nothing in the pockets: Some items, such as lipstick tubes and

Left Behind

As strange as it may sound, some customers are going to leave their laundry with an attendant for wash-and-fold, then walk out the door and never come back. Some will also leave their laundry in the machines, then go run errands and never return. You should hold on to the laundry for a while, but eventually you're going to run out of space.

Make sure you have a sign in your laundry and a notice on your invoices saying that you are not responsible for clothing left in the store after a certain amount of time, such as 30 days. If the laundry was left in a machine, gather the abandoned clothing and place it in a bag marked with the day, time, and machine in which it was left. Unfortunately, you'll need to dry it if it's wet—otherwise it will mold. Then store the clothing in a back room for the length of time you have said you will keep left laundry. After that, give the clothes to a charity. Ask for a receipt for your donation so you can deduct the amount at tax time.

pens, will stain the entire wash. Others, namely cigarette lighters, could explode in a dryer.

- *Wash and dry the laundry.* Follow the directions on clothing labels and make sure dark-colored items (especially those dyed red) are separate from the light-colored ones. Also be sure to keep each customer's laundry separate.
- *Fold the laundry.* Janet H. has all her attendants fold laundry the same way. She feels that her repeat customers become accustomed to having their laundry folded a certain way. "You kind of section your drawer off a certain way," she says, "and if it's folded a different way and it doesn't fit in that spot, that's annoying."
- *Place the laundry in a plastic bag and weigh it again to make sure it weighs the same as it did when the customer brought it in.* This helps ensure that a few shirts or a pair of pants didn't end up in someone else's wash. When the customer comes to pick up the laundry, weigh it again to show him or her that it's all there.

Laundry Invoice

Sunbright Laundry
1000 Washtime Street
Clean Valley, TN 33333
(800) 555-1234

Invoice No.: 5150

Today's date ____________________

Customer name ____

Customer phone ____

Order for pickup on:

S M T W TH F S after ________ A.M./P.M.

Weight ____________ Price ______________ Total ______________

Special instructions or conditions: ______________________________

____

____

Not responsible for items left more than 30 days.

Bright Idea

Asking customers to pay for wash-and-fold service ahead of time ensures that more of them will come back to pick up their laundry. A surprising number of customers never return for their clothes.

Pricing and Turnaround

According to *American Coin-Op* magazine, laundry owners are charging between $.65 and $1.10 a pound for basic wash-and-fold service. However, many owners will charge lower rates to provide incentives, and they'll charge extra for orders with special instructions.

Craig H., who has three laundries in Washington state, for example, charges $.20 less for large orders. Robert G., in Floral Park, New York, charges a lower rate for customers who pay when they drop off their clothes. On the other hand, many laundries charge extra for special instructions, such as cold water only for some items or delicate wash for selected items. You may also want to consider charging more for shirts that need to be placed on hangers or starched.

Wash-and-fold service is pretty speedy: Laundries often have clothes all washed and folded by the evening, provided that customers bring their orders in before noon. Some laundry owners give a one-day turnaround for clothes that require special instructions.

Delivery

While offering wash-and-fold service provides your customers with the convenience they want, delivery takes that service to the next level. In response to customer demand for timesaving services, a few laundry owners are starting to make delivery part of the package. They pick up dirty laundry at customers' homes, take it to their store, wash and fold it, and bring it back the next day.

This service works best for laundries that have a number of interested customers who live in close proximity to each other. "If [laundry owners] can get enough [interested customers] to establish some type of route, they are willing to take on a pickup and drop-off at an additional charge to the customer," says Paul Partyka, editor of *American Coin-Op* magazine. He notes that with so many two-income families, the need for this service is growing. A laundry can expect to earn about $1.50 a pound for delivery service.

Laundries that are located near business parks may find that they have another whole market niche that will be interested in delivery services. Janet H., who offers a wash-and-fold service at her laundry in Fullerton, California, says that she's hoping to start a route for some of the office buildings in her neighborhood. "We'll be putting out flyers in business areas," she says. "We're looking for lots of different things to do to increase business."

Dry Cleaning

Many coin- or card-operated laundry owners also contract with a dry cleaner. They take clothes from customers and hold them for the dry cleaner—who later picks up the clothes, cleans them, and brings them back. Collette C. says a dry-cleaning service approached her and her partner, Kim C., about taking dry-cleaning items. The partners get 30 percent of the profit on each order they take—just for tagging the clothes and storing them for the dry cleaner. Collette says it's a great deal: "We don't do much for that 30 percent."

If you have the room to store dry cleaning in your laundry and you're interested in this service, contact local dry cleaners and see if they are interested. These arrangements are usually beneficial to both you and the dry cleaner. You get a cut of their profits, and they get increased business because it's convenient for customers to bring all their clothes to one place.

Attending Your Laundry

As we mentioned earlier, not all laundry owners hire employees to attend their stores. Some decide they don't need the expense and don't want to spend the time supervising employees; others feel that having attendants makes their store more appealing to customers.

To Attend or Not

Probably the most important reason to hire attendants is to provide better customer service. When someone loses money in a machine, for example, an attendant can immediately issue a refund. Attendants make sure the soap machine is always stocked, the bathroom has toilet paper, and the floor is mopped up after a spill.

"How can you promote your services and have a service mandate if you're unattended?" asks Craig H., owner of three laundries in Washington state. He says that he and his partner didn't even consider running unattended laundries.

Attendants who are friendly make customers feel welcome in your store. Janet H., who has a laundromat in Fullerton, California, says that her customers come to know the attendants and become loyal to them, which keeps them coming back to her laundry. "I felt having someone there was going to give better service to the customers," she says. Janet adds that hiring attendants was definitely the right decision. "Every time I go to my store, somebody says 'I've never seen such a beautiful store; the attendants are so helpful,'" she says. "I know that the attendants' attitude toward the people makes a tremendous amount of difference."

Stat Fact
Roughly half of the laundromats in the United States employ attendants, according to Paul Partyka of *American Coin-Op* magazine, which surveys its readers annually.

With attendants, you can also offer special amenities such as videos for the kids, free coffee, promotional discounts, and wash-and-fold service. Attendants can also help customers use the machinery properly, which helps keep your equipment in good shape. In addition, they can steer customers toward the more profitable machines—front-load washers. Some customers avoid front-loaders because they are not sure how to use them.

Finally, attendants help prevent theft and vandalism. Janet H., who owned several unattended stores before she decided to hire employees, says that customers often kicked and dented her machines, and vandals sometimes torched her change machine. Having an attended laundromat provides a deterrent to these types of crime. "That's why a lot of people do employ attendants," says Brian Wallace of the Coin Laundry Association. Attendants also make customers feel safer in your store, especially at night.

On the other hand, hiring employees adds a whole new dimension to your business. You have to find them, train them, supervise them, and, most importantly, pay them. A few of the laundry owners interviewed for this book decided they wanted to simplify things and go unattended.

Brian D., who owns a laundry in Iowa City, says he thought about hiring someone who could clean for him and do wash-and-fold service, but he decided against it. "I

Team Uniform

Your customers can probably guess that the woman wiping down the machines is an employee at the store, but they might not know that the man doing wash-and-fold is an attendant—he looks like any other customer.

To help your customers know who to ask for help, it's a good idea to give your attendants an identifying marker, such as a T-shirt with your laundry's name or logo. You could also supply your workers with aprons or buttons.

Janet H., who runs a laundry in Fullerton, California, had several T-shirts printed up with her logo—a bee—on the front and the back. All her attendants wear them while they're working, just as she does. "When [customers] come into the store, when they have a problem, they know that the lady with the big bee on her shirt is the one to ask for help," she says.

thought maybe I'd be able to make more with drop-off," he says, "but I didn't want the headache of hiring and supervising an employee." If you've decided otherwise and plan to hire someone to attend your laundry, read on.

Fitting the Description

If you'll be offering a wash-and-fold service, much of your attendants' time will be spent washing your customers' clothes. The job description should also include assisting customers with their laundry and the equipment. Attendants should watch for any customers who seem confused about how to work the machines or who appear to be looking for help. This is especially important if you have a card system. Most customers are used to a coin-operated laundry, but a card laundry might befuddle them enough to send them elsewhere.

"We keep a real close watch on the card machine," says Janet H., who runs a card-operated laundry. "If someone walks in, we go and say 'Can I help you?' If they are at all confused, we say 'Don't worry about it; I'm going to walk you through this.' "

Attendants should ease new customers into your store, says Paul Donovan with PWS. If someone walks in and starts looking around, attendants should say, "'Hi, how are you? Let me show you how the soap works; give me your basket, and I'll run you through the process,'" he says. Part of an attendant's job is just to chat and be friendly

Employee Closing Tasks

It's a good idea to give your employees a checklist to make sure everything gets done before they close for the night. We've compiled a list of the basic tasks your employees will need to perform:

Cleaning

- ❒ Pick up trash off the floor, tables, and seats
- ❒ Sweep and mop the floor
- ❒ Clean dryer lint screens
- ❒ Wipe down all machines
- ❒ Wipe down folding tables
- ❒ Empty wastebaskets
- ❒ Clean restroom
- ❒ Gather carts and place them near washers
- ❒ Wash windows weekly
- ❒ Clean coffeepot

Front Counter

- ❒ Count cash in register
- ❒ Place cash and invoices in a safe place
- ❒ Mark and store forgotten clothes

Supplies

- ❒ Fill all vending machines
- ❒ Restock restroom supplies
- ❒ Check supply inventory
- ❒ Replace any burned-out bulbs

Bright Idea

Station your attendants near the entrance to the store so they can spot any new or confused customers and assist them before they walk out. You may want to have them work behind a counter so it's obvious to customers where they should go for help.

with the customers. Once customers come to know and like the attendants in your store, they'll want to come back and see them.

Your attendants will need to clean, too, and they should clean as soon as there is any kind of mess or spill, rather than wait for closing time. Once the store closes and all the customers are gone, the attendants should thoroughly clean the entire store including the machines, the bathroom, and the floor. See Chapter 2 for more on the specific cleaning tasks that your attendants will need to take care of daily.

If you offer any amenities, such as videos or free lollipops for the children, your attendants will need to keep track of these supplies. And if you serve free coffee or snacks, your attendants will need to keep the coffeepot full and the snacks flowing.

You'll want to collect the money out of the machines and the changer yourself, but you'll have to let your employees take money for wash-and-fold and dry-cleaning orders. Have your employees total the money in the cash register at the end of each day and put it in a safe place, along with the receipts. You can check the invoices against the cash drawer to make sure your employees aren't stealing from you.

Finally, your attendants need to keep track of your inventory of cleaning supplies, wash-and-fold materials, and vending items (if you own the machines). Figure out a system that attendants can use to let you know which supplies are getting low. A dry-erase board in the back room, or even a notepad on the front counter, can do the job. Other duties for your attendants will include:

- Restocking vending machines (if you own the machines)
- Retrieving laundry carts from the parking lot
- Giving refunds on cards or for broken machines
- Marking broken machines so other customers will not use them
- Restocking bathroom supplies
- Emptying trash cans

Shifty Attendants

Most laundries have one attendant on duty at a time, though sometimes attendants' shifts will overlap a few hours during the busiest times of the day. Depending on the hours you are open, and whether you want to hire full- or part-time employees, most likely there will be two to three shifts to cover every day, seven days a week.

> **Don't forget that you'll need an additional employee to help cover weekend shifts**

If your laundry is open from 6 A.M. to 10 P.M. each day, and an attendant spends an extra hour cleaning (until 11 P.M.), that means you have a total of 18 hours a day when you need someone to mind the store. There are a number of ways you could choose to cover these hours. If you only want to hire part-time employees, you could hire three attendants and have each work one six-hour shift a day, with the afternoon shift overlapping the evening shift to cover your busiest time of day.

The employee on the first shift would open the store at 6 A.M., help customers, and do the bulk of the wash-and-fold while business is slowest in the morning. The second-shift attendant would come in at noon and leave at 6 P.M., and would do wash-and-fold until business picks up in the late afternoon. At that point, he or she would then focus on customer service. The employee on the last shift, from 5 to 11 P.M., would assist customers and he or she would do a thorough cleaning after the store closes. Don't forget that you'll need an additional employee to help cover weekend shifts, or you might choose to work some weekend shifts yourself.

Of course, some of your employees could work longer shifts and others shorter shifts. And some could work five days a week and others just a few days a week. The hours and days they work will likely depend on the hours you're open and your employees' availability. If you would prefer to have one or two full-time employees, instead of several part-time employees, your shift schedule will look a little different than the one we've just described. Also factor in the number of shifts that you will be able to work yourself. The more you can work, the more you will save on the cost of employee payroll and benefits.

If you decide not to have an attended laundry, you might still want to hire someone to clean for you. You'll still have to pay their salary, naturally, but since they'll be working only two to three hours a day, the cost to you won't be nearly as much as that of a full-time employee. For a part-time employee making a little above minimum wage, you're looking at about $500 a month as opposed to $1,500 a month in payroll and benefits for a full-time employee.

A few laundry owners have found that retirees make good janitors for their stores because the work is part-time, which suits the modified work schedule that many seniors prefer. Seniors also tend to be experienced and reliable. Dave A., who has an unattended laundry in New Glarus, Wisconsin, does much of the cleaning along with his wife. But they also employ a retiree who cleans four mornings a week. Robert G., who has a laundry in Floral Park, New York, relies on retirees to clean his store before it opens and after it closes.

> **Smart Tip**
> Show prospective hires the "Attendant Training Video" offered by the Coin Laundry Association (see the Appendix for contact information). The video will give them a good idea of the job duties they'll have to perform, and you can weed out those who aren't interested before you hire them.

Hiring Hints

Most of the entrepreneurs interviewed for this book said that they found prospective attendants through their customers. These laundry owners advertised their available positions by putting up signs in their stores. Some of the attendants they hired were in fact customers, while others were friends and acquaintances of customers.

The laundry owners we interviewed said that when hiring attendants they looked for people they thought would be good at handling customers. "They have to like people because they are faced with people all day long," says Janet.

Janet adds that she looks for attendants who have a neat appearance, as they will be cleaning customers' clothes. "I look for someone who's fairly neat about themselves," she says. If the applicant is a customer, she asks her attendants if they have seen the applicant doing his or her laundry. She wants people who treat their laundry with care: "If they don't take pains with their own laundry, they're not going to take pains with other people's laundry," she says.

If many of your customers speak a language other than English, try to hire someone who speaks that language. A Spanish-speaking attendant will help draw those customers who are more comfortable speaking Spanish.

Training Time

The best way to train new employees is to have them work with either an experienced attendant or with you for several days. Walk them through the wash-and-fold procedure, working the cash machine, refilling the vending machines, cleaning the store, and anything else that will be a routine part of their job.

Be sure to talk to new attendants about customer service and let them know what to do when a customer complains. Let your new attendants know what the policy is if a customer wants a free wash after a machine didn't spin out, for example. Also give your new attendants a checklist for closing down the store to make sure everything is cleaned, checked, and stocked on a daily basis.

In addition, you might want to give your attendants some training in equipment maintenance. If your attendants know how to solve problems quickly, that means machines will be up and running—and earning money—more quickly. It also means you won't receive so many frantic phone calls. You can teach them what you know, or you can send them to equipment school—manufacturers offer training sessions for their equipment on a regular basis. Make sure you give your attendants your phone number when you're not at the store so they can reach you if they do have a problem they can't solve.

> **Tip...**
>
> **Smart Tip**
>
> The more time you spend supervising your attendants—visiting the laundry, responding to their requests, and checking on their performance—the less likely they are to steal from you or become frustrated with their job and quit. Don't just hire employees and split: Train them, talk with them, and evaluate their job duties regularly.

What's the Motive?

It's a challenge to inspire laundry attendants to do a great job. Attendants usually make little more than minimum wage—the entrepreneurs we talked to pay their employees anywhere from $6 to $8 an hour. There's also little room for advancement in a small company like a laundry, and there are often no benefits. But the laundry owners interviewed for this book said they gave as much financial incentive as they could afford to.

"We try to move them up a little quickly so we can pay a somewhat decent wage," says Collette C., who owns a laundry in Evans, Colorado. She adds, "We tried to do some really nice bonuses at Christmas time."

Craig H., a laundry owner in Washington state, gives his employees a cut of the profits. "We have an incentive program whereby we give back a share of the income of the laundry to the staff at the end of the month," he says. The incentive adds about $2 an hour to their paychecks. Craig says, "It contributes to the feeling that we're all in this together."

Laundry owners said they also tried to motivate their attendants by providing a fun work atmosphere. "We have fun, and we work right alongside them," Collette says.

Craig H. adds, "We try to build a team spirit with our staff, where we feel like we're striding with them side by side toward a common goal, not like we're cracking a whip or shaking a finger at them constantly."

It's to your advantage to keep employee turnover as low as possible. You won't waste valuable time and money training new attendants over and over again, and you will benefit from the experience that long-term employees gain after they have been on the job for a while. So how can you hang on to your employees? You'll have a head start if you treat them considerately, give them the training they need to do a good job, and offer them as much financial incentive as you can afford.

Promoting Your Store

Now that your laundromat is ready for customers, it's time to do a little advertising. If your store is new, you'll need to introduce it to the community; if you've bought an existing one, you'll want to let customers know the store has a new owner. And if you've been operating for a while, you'll still want to do some advertising to bring in new customers—and hold on to your current ones.

In this chapter, we'll discuss the types of advertising that work for laundromats including opening celebrations, Yellow Pages ads, in-store promotions, and mailers. We'll also cover what's probably the most effective form of advertising—customer service.

Of Advertising and Laundries

Laundry owners are not known for their sophisticated marketing techniques. In fact, says Brian Wallace, executive director of the Coin Laundry Association, "Most coin laundries do no advertising whatsoever." According to Wallace, most owners rely on business from customers who see their store when walking or driving past.

Tim Craig, a former laundry owner and distributor who is now a consultant, even believes that promotions are usually a waste of time and money. "Advertising won't really do you any good," he says. The majority of customers use a laundry because it's convenient, he argues, not because one is better than another. However, some of the entrepreneurs interviewed for this book said they had success with advertising techniques.

If you decide to promote your store, remember that a laundry draws its customers from its immediate neighborhood. You'll want to steer clear of radio, newspapers (unless there is a neighborhood rag), and other media that reach the whole community because you'll spend a lot of money talking to people who will never use your laundry. Focus your marketing efforts on your immediate community: This includes people who live in the vicinity and those who shop or do business near your laundry.

Whatever form of promotion or advertising you decide to go with, make sure you can measure how well it works. If a promotion turns out to be a bomb, you'll want to avoid spending money on it in the future.

Grand Opening

Whether your store is new or you've recently purchased it, a grand opening celebration is a good way to let people know you are in business. One of our entrepreneurs, Collette C., the laundry owner in Colorado, says sales jumped $1,000 in the week after she and her partner, Kim C., held their grand opening.

A grand opening usually involves a big advertising push for a day of opening celebrations at the laundromat. An enormous sign saying "Grand Opening" or a tent in the parking lot will draw in passersby. At the celebration, give prospective customers the chance to win prizes and snack on free food while they tour your recently built or renovated laundromat. If you want to throw a grand opening in a parking lot or on the sidewalk, check with your landlord and the city or county to see if you need a permit.

Brian D., of Iowa City, Iowa, joined forces with neighboring businesses to help promote his laundry. He asked them to give away prizes, such as free coffee or hair

Take a Survey

Your customers are just sitting around your laundry week after week—why not put them to work for you? Each customer has valuable marketing information to offer, so take a survey.

You can ask your customers if a specific promotion, such as a "Single's Night," will help bring in business. You can ask if they would pay more for newer equipment, or if they'd like to have free doughnuts on weekday mornings.

Robert G., who owns a laundry in Floral Park, New York, surveyed his customers about whether they wanted to use a card system or go to the dollar coin. He got his answer and retrofitted his machines to accept dollar coins.

Offer customers something in return for answering the survey, such as a reduced-price wash or a complementary box of soap. You'll get more responses, and you'll get less resentment from people who don't want to give away marketing information for nothing.

cuts, and in return he named them as cosponsors in the advertising. He then took out a one-page ad in the local newspaper to call attention to the grand opening. On the day of the celebration, he put up a tent in the parking lot and gave away cotton candy and popcorn. He held a drawing every half hour to give away the prizes from neighboring businesses, which included free movies, sandwiches, and dry cleaning. "We gave away a couple thousand dollars in prizes," he says. "People loved it. It was real busy."

If many of your prospective customers will be families with children, try to include something in your grand opening that will appeal to kids, such as face painting, a drawing contest, or free toys. Parents are always looking for cheap ways to entertain their offspring.

Run your new laundry for a few months before you have your grand opening to make sure you've ironed out any kinks. Brian D. says he waited about a month before his grand opening. "We got a feel for the machines," he says, "[and] got the bugs worked out of [the store]."

New Kid in Town

When you purchase an existing store—whether or not you renovate it—it's still a good idea to let customers know there's someone new at the helm. In all likelihood, the previous owner wasn't promoting the business or providing top-notch customer service. Why bother when he or she was planning on selling? If customers hear there's a new owner, they may be willing to give the store another try and see what the new owner has to offer.

"You have to let the people know it's under new management," says Robert G., who has purchased three laundries in New York state. "Word gets spread around that there's a new owner in town, and he pays refunds when you lose your money."

You can simply put up a sign saying "New Owner" or "Under New Management." If you've added a coat of paint or made a few minor repairs, customers will already see the difference.

Dollar Stretcher

Have a set of business cards printed for your laundry—you can get 1,000 for as little as $15—and stamp on the back that they're good for a free wash. Distribute them everywhere: Leave them with waiters at restaurants, drop them in mail slots, and hand them to acquaintances.

The Trusty Phone Book

Put yourself in the shoes of a potential customer: You've moved to an apartment in a new community. After a week, you notice that your socks are all dirty, your clothes are a mess from moving, the curtains in your apartment look like they've never been washed—you need to find a laundry fast. What do you do? Most likely, you're going to open the phone book and take a peek under "Laundry."

Laundromats are ideal for Yellow Pages advertising because people just need to find one that's conveniently located, and open the hours they need to do their laundry. In fact, many laundry owners say they've had good success with the Yellow Pages. Janet H., who operates a laundry in Fullerton, California, says that her laundry receives three to four calls a day from her Yellow Pages ad. It helps that hers is the only laundry in the area with a 2-by-2-inch ad. "It's absolutely worth the $86 a month," she says.

If you run an ad in the Yellow Pages, here are a few pointers.

- Make the phone number bold or otherwise easy to see.
- Give directions or cross streets, not just the address.
- List the hours you're open.
- Make sure the type is uncluttered and easy to read.
- Use your logo if you have one.

Brian D. saved some money in his Yellow Pages advertising by taking up just one line. He gave the name of his laundry and added "24 hours," a big plus in his university neighborhood. His answering machine then states the location and repeats that it's open 24 hours a day.

Preaching to the Converted

A rule of thumb in advertising is that it's much cheaper to retain customers than find new ones. You can keep your customers coming back by offering a variety of discounts and in-store promotions.

A common promotion is to offer customers a reduced-price wash during the day on Tuesdays, Wednesdays, and Thursdays. These are the slowest times for most laundries, so it'll help you turn a profit just to have the machines in use. If you have a card system, you can program the machines to draw less money from the cards on those days.

If your machines take coins, you will need an attendant to give customers an extra coin. If a top-loader wash is normally $1.25, and you're offering it at $1, for example, your attendant can give customers a quarter. You can put up a sign saying, "Reduced-price wash! See attendant." Then have your attendant put the money in the machine for the customer—you don't want people coming in for free quarters.

You could also reward your loyal customers with a free wash after so many trips to your laundry. Use a punch card, or stamp the back of a business card. Some laundries reward their wash-and-fold customers by charging a lower price for dropping off bigger loads of laundry.

> **Bright Idea**
>
> If you have a super-size washer, advertise it to the residents in the neighborhood where you have your store. Advertise even to those who wouldn't normally use a laundry. If you point out that it can wash large comforters, drapes, and even rugs, you might pull in some extra business.

Robert G. sends out a flyer with refund slips to his customers once a year. He'll give them a special, such as $.50 off their next wash. "They seem to get a kick out of that," he says. "It makes them feel special."

Some laundry owners try to draw in customers by offering free goodies in their stores. Janet H. offers candy for the kids (with the parents' OK, of course) and free coffee; Collette C. also has free coffee available in her store.

Ideas that Worked—and Didn't

Every laundry and every neighborhood is different. What works like gangbusters for one laundry owner may fall flat for another, so it's difficult to generalize about the sort of marketing strategies that will work best for you. But here are a few tactics that worked for the entrepreneurs we interviewed.

- Craig H., in Washington state, has had success including his stores in "welcome to the neighborhood" packets that his local chamber of commerce sends to new residents.

- Dave A., who runs a laundry in a tourist town in Wisconsin, gets some vacationers' business by being included on a town map for tourists.
- Collette C. has had many customers respond to her "buy one wash—get one free" direct mailer.

On the flip side, here are some tactics that didn't work at all.

- Janet H. found that doorknob hangers, those paper hangers with a printed logo or phone number on them, were expensive to have made and brought in very little extra business.
- Collette C. tried advertising on the back of grocery coupons—with very little luck.

Tip...

Smart Tip

Try offering free soap to your customers on certain days of the week or for special promotions. Buy detergent in bulk and hand it out in plastic cups—this is much cheaper than handing out individual boxes.

Word-of-Mouth

The best advertising is also the cheapest. If you have a nice, clean store with friendly attendants and working equipment, your customers are going to tell their friends and family members about it. In other words, the best way to promote your store is to offer great customer service. "Word-of-mouth works best," says Dave A. in New Glarus, Wisconsin. "If you keep it clean, and people like the location, they'll tell people."

The laundry owners we spoke with said they try to provide top-quality customer service by keeping their laundry clean and in working condition at all times, by offering entertainment for adults and their children, and by being friendly and helpful. They also said it's important to be attentive to customers' needs. For example, Collette

Lucky Logos

Think about developing a logo for your store. A logo, usually a simple picture or symbol, will come to represent your laundry and help you market it. Logos are often more recognizable than names.

You can use your logo in your store, on attendants' uniforms, on the signs outside and on your delivery truck (if you have one). A logo is also a great advertisement to include on any marketing material, such as flyers, business cards, or coupons. Establish a standard of quality in your store, and customers will start associating your logo with quality. And if you want to expand, the logo will help customers easily recognize that you've opened an extension of the old store.

C. in Evans, Colorado, says that some of her customers have started visiting her laundry because other laundry owners kicked them out when the store closed—even though their wash wasn't finished. "You just don't do that," she says.

Dollar Stretcher

If you have a computer, print out some flyers offering a reduced-price wash or dry. Place them on the windshields of cars in the parking lots near your store since people who run chores in the area are likely to use your laundry.

Janet H. learned the importance of customer service once she hired attendants. Her business has increased markedly, even though she charges a little more than the competition. "We just bend over backward to give them the kind of service to warrant that," she says.

Collette C. concurs: "Get to know your customers and let them feel like you really appreciate their business," she says. "Provide them with something to do. There's nothing more boring than sitting in a laundromat. Make it a fun place. A lot of our feedback has been that it's really fun to come here. It feels like home."

Craig H. adds that customers want respect and a fair shake from the laundry. "We want our customers to feel like they are being treated with dignity and that they get value from us," he says. "When we make a mistake, we try and fix it."

Once you have opened your business and started getting the word out to customers that yours is the best laundry in town, you'll need to get back to the books and see how well your business is coming along. In the next chapter, we'll look at accounting for laundromats—how to keep the books, price the services, and make sure you're turning a profit.

11

Counting the Coins

We have already discussed how much you can expect to pay just to open a store, but what will it cost you to keep it running successfully? And what kind of profit can you expect to make from your store? In this chapter, we're going to show you how to keep track of the money you have coming in and going out each month. We'll take a look at what your monthly bookkeeping will be like, and how to approach pricing and filing taxes.

Managing the Bottom Line

Managing your finances is crucial because you must know how your business—every aspect of it—is doing. If you are on top of your income and expenses, you can discover whether you're offering your services at the right price. You can also assess whether your wash-and-fold service justifies the cost of a second employee, or if you can afford to pay a janitor to do the cleaning. In addition, you can see how much you're spending on repairs to gauge when it's time to buy new equipment.

Ultimately, when you add up the numbers you can see if the laundry business is even working out for you—or if it's time to sell. You also need to track your income carefully so you have something to report at tax time. We'll get to this topic a little later in the chapter.

Incoming

One of the realities of owning a laundry business (especially if yours is a coin laundry) is that there are lots of bills and coins to count. Other entrepreneurs, take consultants for example, will usually earn a few large checks a month that they can just toss in the bank, holding on to the pay stubs for their records. As a laundry owner, however, you will need to count every coin and bill that comes into your store.

In Chapter 2, we drew up a chart that shows you how to keep track of the money each type of equipment or service brings in (see "Equipment Use Chart" on page 19). As we mentioned, this information will help you decide which machines and services are the most popular in your store, but it will also give you a complete daily or weekly income statement. Add to the chart any services you offer—wash-and-fold, dry-cleaning drop-off/pickup, and snack vending—and you will have an accurate picture of the money you are taking in.

While you may want to keep track of your income on a daily or weekly basis, since that's how you collect money, you'll also want to know what your income is on a monthly basis so you can determine your net income. Many of your expenses—utilities, rent, insurance—are charged by the month, so you will need to calculate your income and operating expenses monthly.

Using an accounting program such as Microsoft Money or Intuit QuickBooks will save you time. The Coin Laundry Association also sells an accounting program designed specifically for laundry owners (see the Appendix). Each of these programs costs between $150 and $250. If you use a card system, remember that much of your income will be calculated for you automatically by the system software.

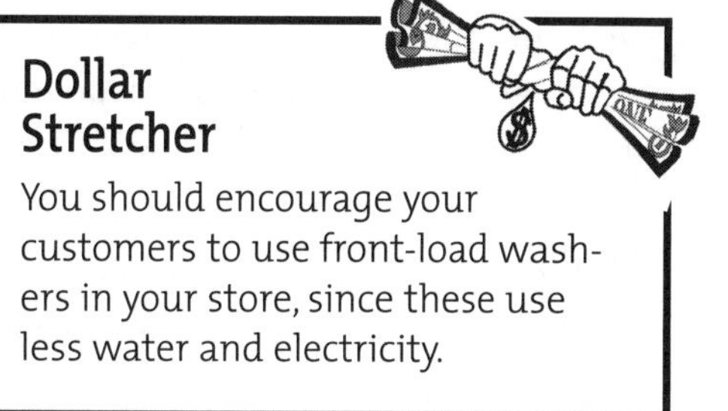

Dollar Stretcher

You should encourage your customers to use front-load washers in your store, since these use less water and electricity.

Let's walk through the ins and outs of determining your gross monthly income. This amount will depend on how much you charge for your machines and how many customers are using them. Most laundromats are charging close to $1 to $1.25 a wash for top-loaders. Front-loaders that can handle up to 18 pounds of laundry run about $1.50 a wash, 25-pounders cost from $2 to $2.50 a wash, 30-pounders cost between $2 and $3.50 a wash; and 35-pounders cost from $2.50 to $3.50 a wash. Dryers usually cost $.25 for a predetermined amount of time, usually 8 to 12 minutes.

Once you decide how much you'll be charging, you can easily figure out what your income will be if you know how many times each piece of equipment is used each day. You can't know that in advance, but according to *American Coin-Op* magazine, an average figure is about four times, or turns per day (TPD). If you multiply the amount you charge for each type of machine by four and add those numbers, you'll have a rough idea of how much you can expect to earn from self-service. You may be able to determine a more exact figure by consulting with your distributor, a consultant, or other laundry owners in your area.

For wash-and-fold service, laundry operators charge customers by the pound, between $.50 and $1.15 is average. The amount of wash-and-fold work you can expect differs, depending on where you are located and how great the demand is for this convenience. If your laundry is located in a relatively wealthy area, you can expect more revenue from wash-and-fold work. Residents in lower-income areas aren't likely to be able to afford drop-off service to the same degree.

Finally, you have to take into account revenue from vending machines (snack and soda machines, as well as soap dispensers). The amount these machines bring in depends on how much business you do. A very small store will earn only $125 or so a year, a very large one as much as $4,000.

To calculate sample monthly income figures, we are going to revisit our two hypothetical laundry businesses: Suds-Are-Us and Squeaky Clean. The "Income and Operating Expenses" worksheet on page 112 shows the monthly revenue for Suds-Are-Us, with an itemized list of calculations for each machine type or service. This figure is an estimate of the *gross* monthly income; you will not have the net income until monthly expenses have been deducted (we will get to this in the next section).

Suds-Are-Us will have revenue from wash-and-fold service, dry-cleaning drop off and pickup, vending machines, and washers and dryers. We will assume 100 pounds of wash-and-fold service a day, at $.90 a pound. We've predicted a TPD of four for calculating the gross monthly income from washing machines and dryers. Top-loaders will cost $1.10 a wash, the 25-pound front-loaders $2.75 a wash, and the 50-pound front-loaders $4.25 a wash. The dryers, costing $.27 for ten minutes, will run an average of 50 minutes each load, for a total of $1.35 a load. To calculate revenue, we'll multiply the following:

Number of machines x TPD x Price per load x Days in a month (30)

The gross monthly income for Squeaky Clean is also shown in the worksheet on page 112. Since Squeaky Clean is an unattended laundry, the only revenue sources will be vending services and washers and dryers. We've also predicted a TPD of four for this business. The top-loaders will cost $1.25 a wash, the 25-pound front-loaders $3.25 a wash, and the 50-pound front-loader $4.50 a wash. The dryers, costing $.25 for ten minutes, will run an average of 50 minutes each load, for a total of $1.25 a load. Again, we've multiplied the number of machines by the TPD by the price for each load by the number of days in a month (which we've assumed to be 30).

Outgoing

Now that you've got an idea of what your income will look like, let's take a look at the kinds of monthly expenses you will encounter as the owner of a laundry business.

The rent will vary widely based on where you are in the country. An urban setting in a high-rent area such as Manhattan or San Francisco is going to cost you as much as $3 a square foot every month, or $6,000 a month for an average-size (2,000-square-foot) laundry. Lower-rent areas could be $1 a square foot every month or less. The rent may or may not include the maintenance fees for landscaping, parking lot upkeep, snow removal, taxes and so on.

Utilities—gas, water, sewer, and electric—are often the biggest expenses for laundromats. Let's say you have 40 washers and 40 dryers, which is probably typical for an average- to large-size laundry. Depending on what your utility company charges, you are going to pay between $2,000 and $4,000 a month. This amount will also depend on how much use your machines get. The good news is that the more you're paying in utilities, the more you'll be making in revenue.

Dollar Stretcher

Ask your utility company if you can get a discount because you're a good customer. Suggest that you have some tempting offers from other companies, but that you'd like to keep using the current company. Often, utility companies will offer a small discount.

You'll also need insurance to cover you for damage (theft, fire, flood) and liability (slip-and-fall or other claims from customers). The cost of insurance is hard to generalize because it's based on so many factors: location, size of the laundry, whether it's attended, whether you have a security system, the hours you're open, how much coverage you want, and whether you want business interruption coverage. Insurance costs can range between $100 and $400 a month for a policy that covers damage and liability.

Paying your employees and providing benefits will be another big cost. Laundry attendants earn wages that are slightly above the minimum wage, somewhere around $6 to $10 an hour. Let's say you pay $6.75 a hour, and your employees work a collective total of 420 hours a month. That means your payroll will be $2,835 a month, just for hourly wages. You'll have to pay more—about $1,500 a month—for workers' compensation, social security, and benefits, should you choose to offer them.

It's easy to remember the biggies—utilities, rent, salaries—but those little expenses add up, too. Miscellaneous expenses—soap, cleaning supplies, invoices for wash-and-fold, toilet paper, etc.—will cost you between $200 and $1,000 a month. Equipment repairs will depend on how old your machines are. If they're new, they're covered under warranty if anything goes wrong. But if they're five years old and out of warranty, you can expect to pay from $500 to $1,000 a month for parts and labor for a store with 40 machines.

Take another look at the "Income and Operating Expenses" worksheet on page 112 to view the operating costs incurred by our two hypothetical laundry businesses. To calculate the monthly expenses for Suds-Are-Us, we have assumed that the owner pays his three employees $6.75 an hour, and that $1.50 per square foot every month is the going rate for rent (for the 3,000-square-foot store). Since Suds-Are-Us is newly constructed, we've also taken into account that the equipment is new, still under warranty, and requires no upkeep.

Squeaky Clean, on the other hand, employs no attendants, and the rental cost is $2 a square foot every month (for a 1,000-square-foot space). Since the owner bought an existing laundry, we're also assuming that the equipment is five years old and that the warranty has expired (so there are monthly repair costs to cover). The owner did buy three new machines, which are covered under a parts and service warranty.

To arrive at a figure for net monthly income, simply subtract monthly operating expenses from gross monthly income. The net monthly incomes for our two hypothetical laundries are found at the bottom of the "Income and Operating Expenses" worksheet.

The Bottom Line

As we mentioned, you'll need to know your income and expenses in excruciating detail for tax purposes. If, heaven forbid, the IRS decides to audit you, you must be able to substantiate your expenses.

Income and Operating Expenses

Income and operating expense calculations for Suds-Are-Us are based on 30 top-load washers ($1.10 a wash), 12 25-pound front-loaders ($2.75 a wash), three 50-pound front-loaders ($4.25 a wash), and 16 stacked dryers (32 individual dryers, at $1.35 a load). Suds-Are-Us also has revenue coming in from vending services. And since Suds-Are-Us is attended, wash-and-fold service and dry-cleaning drop off/pickup are also sources of revenue.

Squeaky Clean has 10 top-loaders ($1.25 a wash), four 25-pound front-loaders ($3.25 a wash), one 50-pound front-loader ($4.50 a wash), and 6 stacked dryers (12 dryers, at $1.25 a load). Vending service is the only other source of revenue since this laundry is unattended.

Sources of Monthly Revenue	Suds-Are-Us	Squeaky Clean
Top-loaders (# washers x 4 TPD x price x 30 days)	$3,960	$1,500
25-pound front-loaders (# washers x 4 TPD x price x 30 days)	3,960	1,560
50-pound front-loaders (# washers x 4 TPD x price x 30 days)	1,530	540
Dryers (# dryers x 4 TPD x price x 30 days)	5,184	1,800
Vending	1,400	540
Wash-and-fold: 100 lbs. x $.90 x 30 days	2,700	0
Dry-cleaning drop off/pickup	500	0
Gross Monthly Income	**$19,234**	**$5,940**
Monthly Expenses		
Rent	$4,500	$2,000
Utilities	3,700	1,350
Insurance	400	100
Advertising/promotions	150	0
Payroll (with taxes and overtime)	4,000	0
Repairs	0	350
Loan payment	1,500	500
Miscellaneous expenses	750	250
Total Monthly Expenses	**$15,000**	**$4,550**
NET MONTHLY INCOME	**$4,234**	**$1,390**

You'll be able to figure out your own projected net income once you find a potential location for your laundromat (see Chapter 3) and have chosen a distributor (see Chapter 6). With these basics in place, you'll have a much better idea of what your projected monthly expenses will be like. In addition, you'll be able to determine your rent, utility rates, and any sewer connection fees that you may have to pay.

> **Bright Idea**
>
> Price your front-load washers so they offer a better value than top-loaders. Twenty-five-pound front-loaders can hold three loads, for example, so price them less than three times the cost of using top-loaders. If you charge $1.25 a wash for a top-loader, charge $3.25 a wash for a 25-pounder.

The distributor can tell you how many and what types of machines you'll want to install, and the equipment manufacturer can tell you how much gas, electricity, and water the equipment will use. Once you have a location, you can also get an estimate on insurance. Add employees' salaries (if you'll be hiring any), miscellaneous expenses, and the monthly payments on your loan, and you'll have your monthly costs.

The big question, of course, is how much you'll make. To be on the safe side when you calculate your projected monthly income, you may want to assume that your equipment does only three turns a day. Make another conservative estimate for what you'll make from wash-and-fold, dry cleaning, and vending income each month. Add these figures and subtract your expenses from your income—then you will have your projected net monthly income. Before you sign a lease, and before you buy any equipment, make sure that the net is something you can live with.

The Price Is Right

Setting a price for your equipment and services can be a little tricky. You can charge only as much as customers are willing to pay. And you have to consider the fact that if you raise prices, some of your customers may visit your competitor down the street.

Intense competition in some parts of the country has kept top-loader prices as low as $.50 per wash; operators who charge such a low price are barely making a profit. Laundry experts caution against worrying too much about the competition. If you charge so little you're losing money, you might as well close up shop. Charging impossibly low prices just keeps the whole industry down, adds Paul Partyka of *American Coin-Op* magazine.

Besides, a store that charges a higher price has more money to spend on the amenities and services that bring customers back, such as working televisions, functioning equipment, and clean floors. Brian D., who runs a laundry in Iowa City, Iowa, says he's planning on raising his top-loader prices from $1.25 to $1.50 a wash. That would make his laundry the most expensive in the area. "I'm wary of being the first to raise

> **Smart Tip**
> Tip...
> Be sure to put up signs letting customers know about any price increases. You don't want them wondering why the machines won't start or why the dryer stopped so early.

rates," he admits. But he adds that the extra amenities he offers justify the price increase. "I'm offering good quality equipment, good quality water [because of a water softener that he installed], and good drying."

Andrew Cunningham, a former laundry owner and a laundry consultant, offers one tactic to avoid intense competition: If everyone else is charging $.75 a wash for a top-load washer, and that price is too low for you to make a profit, put in all front-loaders. "Avoid the argument altogether," he says. This may not work for your laundry, but you could emphasize your front-loaders rather than top-loaders.

Finally, if you raise your prices, you might find that your competitors follow suit. According to the *Western States Coin Laundry News*, one laundry owner in an area with intense competition bit the bullet, jacked up his prices, and found that all his competitors raised theirs to the same amount.

Whether you have a card system or coin-operated machines, you can change prices relatively easily. For a card system and newer coin machines, you program in a new price. For older machines with slide systems, you change the number of slots that are open in the slide. Slide machines typically have eight quarter-slots—if you charge $1 a wash, you open four of the slots. To increase the price, you open up one more slot. Then, if you find you're losing too many customers, you can always switch back.

Tax Time

April 15th is the one time of the year you'll have a leg up on consultants and other low-overhead entrepreneurs. You will have lots and lots of deductions. Everything you buy for your laundry, from washing machines to paint for the restroom, is a deduction. Rent, utilities, paychecks, and insurance are obvious, but don't forget all those little deductions, including the paper you buy for flyers you distribute in the parking lot, association dues, even flowers you bring to your store to freshen it up.

Here are a number of tax deductions that, as a laundry owner, you should not overlook:

- *A home office.* If you use some part of your home for your administrative tasks, you may qualify for a deduction. However, it must be a space solely dedicated to your business.
- *Mileage between laundries.* This may apply if you own more than one store; however, you may not deduct the miles from home to your laundry. You can deduct mileage when you travel to buy supplies or parts.

- *Clothing left behind.* If you donate the clothing that customers leave in your store, you may be able to deduct the value of the clothes on your tax return. When you donate the items to charity, ask for a receipt for tax purposes.
- *City licenses or fees.* The sewer connection fees you'll have to pay when you open your laundry are tax deductible, in addition to any other business licenses you have to purchase.
- *Refunds.* The money that you refund to customers who lost (or claimed they lost) money in your machines is also deductible—as long as you weren't able to recover the money in a machine.
- *Counterfeits.* You may be able to deduct any slugs or counterfeit bills that end up in your machines. Hold on to these in case you are audited.
- *Office equipment.* You can deduct the computer equipment you buy for accounting purposes.
- *Phone calls.* These are deductible if you make business-related calls from home.
- *Business-related publications.* You may also deduct the cost of subscriptions for any industry-related magazines and newsletters.

Beware!

Don't throw away your receipts once you've filed your tax returns. For equipment that you depreciate, you want to hold on to the receipts for at least as long as the depreciation—likely five years. Five years after that is even better, since the IRS may still ask for your receipts.

Sales Taxes, Too?

Some states charge coin laundries sales taxes on their services. As of 2000, these states include Washington, New Mexico, Iowa, Hawaii, Louisiana, and West Virginia. Wisconsin charges tax on card-operated laundries only, since its laws state that coin-operated laundries are exempt.

The national Coin Laundry Association, its affiliates, and other regional associations are fighting the sales tax. They are arguing that: laundries provide a basic health service, such as food and medicine, so they should not be taxed; most customers of self-service laundries are lower-income, so they can't afford the tax; and coin laundry owners already pay taxes on their equipment when they purchase it.

Laundry associations have hired lobbyists and have had some success in changing these laws so that self-service laundries are excluded. If you're in one of the states affected by the sales tax, and you want to help fight it, contact your local coin laundry association.

Your major equipment—washers, dryers, and water heating systems—may be depreciated over five years. This lets you spread out the expense and the deductions over that time. Alternatively, in some circumstances you may be able to deduct as much as $20,000 of your equipment expenses in one year, rather than depreciate it over five years. You may find that this is advantageous, depending on your tax bracket.

Laundry owners may also qualify for some tax credits. These are even better than deductions because the money you spend is subtracted from your total tax bill. Renovating your laundry to comply with the Americans with Disabilities Act can give you a tax credit. If you put in front-load washers and stacked dryers, both of which are accessible to customers in wheelchairs, you may qualify for this tax credit.

Hiring disadvantaged employees—such as a recipient of Aid to Families with Dependent Children, an ex-felon, a high-risk youth, a veteran, or someone in vocational rehabilitation—may qualify you for a tax credit. If you plan to go this route, you should know that the credit applies only for the first year of hire, and that the employee must work at least 400 hours during that year.

Check with an accountant or tax specialist to verify that you are qualified for the tax deductions and credits you plan to claim. Tax laws can change, and your accountant should be able to tell you what is a legitimate deduction and what isn't.

12

Staying on Top

Now that we've covered the basics of starting a laundry business, and running the day-to-day and month-to-month operations, it's time to turn to some troubleshooting. In this closing chapter, we'll discuss several of the potential problems that you should prepare for as the owner of a laundry, including vandalism, theft, and lawsuits. We'll also offer some ideas on how to reduce utility costs and maximize your income. In short, we'll look at the factors that will enhance your success in the laundry business.

Vandals and Thieves

Vandalism and theft frequently pose problems for owners of unattended laundries, particularly when those laundries are located in rough neighborhoods. The laundry owners interviewed for this book say they've had vandals do a variety of damage to their stores: torching change machines, damaging washers and dryers, throwing a laundry cart through a plate-glass window, and stealing a TV remote control.

Occasionally, a clever thief will get hold of a key for the coin boxes on washers and dryers, or for the bill changer, and start removing the cash. According to the *Western States Coin Laundry News*, one laundry owner realized someone had been skimming coins from the machines after a customer mentioned how nice his "employee" was. The thief had the foresight to take a little bit each time to avoid being discovered.

Many laundry owners avoid the theft and vandalism problem by hiring attendants. Other laundry owners use security cameras and let their customers know they're being watched. Brian D. of Iowa City put a positive spin on the security cameras placed around his store. He wanted to let customers know they were being taped, but rather than saying, "Watch yourself—we're taping you," his signs say, "Security cameras for your protection." Brian says, "It's keeping people pretty much on the straight and narrow."

By collecting money frequently and varying the time you pull coins from your machines, you can help to avoid theft (as discussed in Chapter 2). You'll also know that someone is stealing if you find that the number of coins in your coin boxes doesn't add up—if you charge $1 a wash, for example, and the coins total $3.75.

Staying out of Court

Another reason to hire attendants or add security cameras is to avoid "slip-and-fall" lawsuits or other personal injury claims. Someone who tries to make a bogus claim won't get very far if attendants are on hand or if video cameras are hooked up to record the nonincident.

> Tip...
>
> **Smart Tip**
>
> Keep your video surveillance camera tapes as long as possible: Customers who claim they've been injured in your store have up to a year to file a personal injury lawsuit.

Brian Wallace, executive director of the Coin Laundry Association, said that while laundries are no more prone to these types of lawsuits than other stores, the lawsuits do occur. He adds that 90 percent of claims against laundries are of the slip-and-fall variety, and that a high percentage of those are fraudulent.

If you or an attendant sees a customer fall or become injured in your store, make a careful record of what happened and what conditions in the store led to the accident (if any). If you have security cameras in your store, keep the videotape.

If a lawyer contacts you regarding a claim, contact your insurance agent immediately. He or she can advise you on how to handle the situation. It's generally best not to give the lawyer any additional information until you have spoken with your insurance agent personally.

The best way to avoid lawsuits is to make sure your store is a safe place to do laundry. The fact that someone was hurt in your store doesn't necessarily make you liable—you're liable only if you neglect to create a safe environment. If you have a store that has loose tiles that customers can trip over, and pools of water that can cause customers

Risk Prevention Checklist

To help protect yourself against lawsuits, you'll need to guard against hazards. Use this checklist to identify some of the potential risks to your customers. There may be additional hazards unique to your store, so you should discuss safety issues with your distributor or consultant.

Outside the store

- ❒ Repair or mark any cracks or holes in the sidewalk outside your store.
- ❒ Mark plate-glass windows so customers won't walk through them.
- ❒ Clearly mark any steps into your store and inside the laundromat.

Inside the store

- ❒ Install slip-proof flooring.
- ❒ Make sure the floor is clear of debris.
- ❒ Immediately fix any broken tiles or holes in the floor.
- ❒ Buy cones or signs that say "Wet floor," and use them when cleaning.
- ❒ Use bright lighting, but be sure it doesn't cause glare.
- ❒ Be sure your equipment is working properly.
- ❒ Clearly mark broken machines.
- ❒ Cover or repair any rough or sharp edges on equipment.
- ❒ Lock any closets or back rooms containing cleaning equipment and solutions.
- ❒ Teach your attendants how to respond in an emergency.
- ❒ Install enough fire extinguishers.
- ❒ Clearly mark an emergency exit.

Beware!
Read your water meter on a daily or weekly basis to find out what's normal for your store. Also compare the water usage against your income. If the water meter stays the same, but income drops, there may be a leak somewhere, or someone may be stealing from you.

to slip, you're going to have a harder time fighting a lawsuit successfully. Wallace advises, "You need to keep the store well-maintained and in good working condition."

The Bottom Line

When you are looking for ways to increase your income, don't just look at growing your customer base. While a big group of happy customers will keep you running to the bank, you can also increase your net profit by reducing costs.

Your laundromat has fixed expenses that you can't change, such as rent and insurance. But it also has variable expenses that can change such as salaries, supplies, and utilities. It's worth taking a look at your variable expenses to see if there's a way to increase your profits.

The area with possibly the greatest potential for reducing costs is utilities—one of your largest, if not the largest, expense you'll have. If you take a look around your laundry, you may find several ways to reduce your utility bills. Here are some ideas to get you started:

- *Try lowering the temperature of your water heater.* Most laundry owners keep their water at about 150° Fahrenheit, but you may find your customers are just as happy with a lower temperature.
- *Make sure your dryer vents are clean.* Clogged vents lower the efficiency of dryers, causing them to use more energy. A chimney sweep can clean the vents for you.
- *Look at the flame on your gas dryers.* If the flame is yellow and flickering, gas is being wasted; the flame should be bright blue and should rise straight up. Contact your gas company to adjust the flame—many will do this free of charge.
- *Insulate your water tank.* If your tank wasn't insulated when you purchased or built your laundromat, have your contractor do it now.
- *Inspect your water lines to make sure that you don't have a leak somewhere and that your meter isn't attached to a neighbor's system.* Otherwise, you could be paying for the water of the restaurant next door.
- *Put your lights on timers.* You can turn off those lights that are right next to windows during daylight hours. At night, when the laundry is closed, keep on only those lights you need for security, such as the ones above the change machine and near the door.

- *Consider the efficiency of your machines.* If you have older washers that use more energy and water than newer ones, replacing them may save you more in the long run.

Keys to Success

The key to a successful laundromat can be summed up in two words: customer service. Provide an atmosphere that customers appreciate, make customers and employees feel appreciated, and keep equipment in good working condition. Although the competition in some areas is tight, if you offer good customer service, you can often win over customers from other less-inspired laundromats. If your laundry has an atmosphere that's more fun and your attendants are friendly, your customers will keep returning because they'll feel more comfortable there.

In our interviews with laundry owners and experts for this book, one other point became clear to us. Laundry owners who spend time in their stores getting to know customers and who supervise their attendants closely, reap the most from the business—both financially and personally. Owners who visit their stores only to collect money and wipe down a few machines make less money and tend to dislike the business more than owners who have a greater sense of commitment.

Drought Days

Many parts of the country face water restrictions when a drought occurs. If water customers have restrictions to comply with, laundromats will feel the effect. The good news is that business often increases during a drought. Many people who have their own laundry equipment will use self-service laundries to reduce their home water use. They'll save the water to keep their lawns alive and to enjoy long showers. Apartment complexes may also close their laundry facilities in order to reach water reduction requirements.

The bad news is that local water boards may penalize laundromats for using more water, despite the fact that doing so would be counterproductive. Equipment in laundromats is usually more water efficient than home or apartment machinery.

If your area has been suffering through a drought and water restrictions are going to be implemented, link up with other laundry owners and try to approach your water board before it votes to issue penalties. Also enlist help from your local coin laundry association.

In short, the more you put into your business, the more you will get out of it. With commitment, your laundry will be a business that not only creates a tidy profit for you but that also gives you a sense of enjoyment and the satisfaction of a job well-done. So what are you waiting for? Take what you've learned in these pages and get started on your new venture as a laundry professional!

Appendix
Coin-Operated Laundry Resources

They say you can never be rich enough or young enough. While these could be argued, we believe you can never have enough resources. Therefore, we're giving you a wealth of sources to check into, check out, and harness for your own personal information blitz.

These sources are tidbits—ideas to get you started on your research. They are by no means the only sources out there, and they should not be taken as the ultimate answer. We have done our research, but businesses do tend to move, change, fold, and expand. As we have repeatedly stressed, do your homework. Get out there and start investigating!

As an additional tidbit to get you going, we strongly suggest the following: If you haven't yet joined the Internet Age, do it! Surfing the Net is like waltzing through a library, with a breathtaking array of resources literally at your fingertips.

Associations

Coin Laundry Association, 1315 Butterfield Road, #212, Downers Grove, IL 60515, (630) 963-5547, www.coinlaundry.org (The Coin Laundry Association also has affiliated regional organizations.)

California Coin Laundry Association, P.O. Box 39277, Downey, CA 90239, (562) 861-6106, www.coinlaundromat.com

International Fabricare Institute (organization for dry cleaners, wet cleaners and launderers), 12251 Tech Road, Silver Spring, MD 20904, (301) 622-1900, www.ifi.org

Books

Don Aslett's Stain-Buster's Bible: The Complete Guide to Spot Removal, Don Aslett, Penguin USA

Entrepreneur's business start-up guide No. 1811, *Starting Your Own Business*, Entrepreneur Media Inc., www.smallbizbooks.com

How to Clean Practically Anything, Edward Kippel, Consumer Reports Books

How to Get a Small Business Loan: A Banker Shows You Exactly What to Do to Get a Loan (Small Business Series No. 1), Bryan E. Milling, Sourcebooks Trade

Knock-Out Marketing, Jack Ferreri, Entrepreneur Media Inc., www.smallbizbooks.com

Where to Go When the Bank Says No: Alternatives for Financing Your Business, David R. Evanson, Bloomberg Press

Consultants

Lionel Bogut, 26836 Cherry Hills Blvd., Sun City, CA 92586, (909) 301-7644

Tim Craig, 4 Lavington Road, Hilton Head Island, SC 29928, (843) 686-4664

Andrew Cunningham, Cunningham Consultants, 3812 Sepulveda Blvd., Torrance, CA 90505, (310) 375-3323

Richard Weisinger, CPA, 440 Western Ave., #201, Glendale, CA 91202, (818) 546-1094

Demographics Services

Claritas, 5375 Mira Sorrento Place, #400, San Diego, CA 92121, (800) 866-6510 ext. 650, www.claritas.com

Geonomics, 44 Broomfield Street, #408, Boston, MA 02108, (617) 451-2520, www.geonomicsinc.com

Distributors

IPSO of NY LaunderCenter, 1731 W. Farms Rd., Bronx, NY 10460, (800) 463-4067, www.ipsony.com

Mac-Gray, 22 Water Street, Cambridge, MA 02141, (800) 622-4729, www.mac-gray.com

PWS Inc., 6300 Flotilla Street, Los Angeles, CA 90040, (323) 721-8832, www.pwslaundry.com

Super Laundry, 3021 International Street, Columbus, OH 43228, (800) 346-0892, www.superlaundry.com

Magazines and Newsletters

American Coin-Op, 500 N. Dearborn Street, Chicago, IL 60610-4901, (312) 337-7700

Coin Laundry Newsletter, California Coin Laundry Association, P.O. Box 39277, Downey, CA 90239, (562) 861-6106, www.coinlaundromat.com

The Journal, 1315 Butterfield Road, #212, Downers Grove, IL 60515, (630) 963-5547, e-mail: journal@coinlaundry.org

New Era Magazine, 22031 Bushard Street, Huntington Beach, CA 92646, (714) 962-1351

Western States Coin Laundry News, 26836 Cherry Hills Blvd., Sun City, CA 92586, (909) 301-7644, e-mail: clnews@inland.net

Manuals

California Coin Laundry Association Owner's Manual, P.O. Box 39277, Downey, CA 90239, (562) 861-6106, www.coinlaundromat.com

California Coin Laundry Association Reference Manual, P.O. Box 39277, Downey, CA 90239, (562) 861-6106, www.coinlaundromat.com

Manufacturers

Aaxon (sells machine parts), 5300 NW 12th Avenue, Fort Lauderdale, FL 33309, (954) 772-2100, www.aaxon.com

Hamilton (sells coin changers), P.O. Box 963, Holland, OH 43528, (419) 867-4858

Howard Enterprises (sells miscellaneous laundry equipment, such as wash-and-fold bags, scales, folding tables, and chairs), P.O. Box 3807, Harrisburg, PA 17105, (800) 233-7175

Partsking.com (an online store for machine parts), (800) 462-4814, www.partsking.com

R&B Wire Products (sells laundry carts), 3100 S. Fairview, Santa Ana, CA 92704, (800) 634-0555, www.rbwire.com

Vend-Rite (sells start-up kit for a wash-and-fold service including signs, advertising handouts, invoices, cash tally sheets, and laundry bags), 2555 West Armitage, Chicago, IL 60647, (800) 777-1802

Successful Coin Laundry Owners

Alpine Laundry, Dave and Kris Anderson, 16 14th Ave., New Glarus, WI 53574, (608) 527-2690

The Last Load, Collette Clarkson and Kim Clarkson, 3230 23rd Ave., #100, Evans, CO 80620, (970) 339-9210

Laundromania, Brian De Coster, 737 Mormontrek, Iowa City, IA 52246, (319) 337-7368

Videotapes

Coin Laundry Association Attendant Training Video, Coin Laundry Association, 1315 Butterfield Road, #212, Downers Grove, IL 60515, (630) 963-5547, www.coinlaundry.org

How to Buy a Coin Laundry, California Coin Laundry Association, P.O. Box 39277, Downey, CA 90239, (562) 861-6106, www.coinlaundromat.com

How to Operate a Coin Laundry, California Coin Laundry Association, P.O. Box 39277, Downey, CA 90239, (562) 861-6106, www.coinlaundromat.com

Web Sites

Coinwash.com (a bulletin board of laundries for sale around the country), www.coin wash.com

The Coin Laundry Owners Forum (a bulletin board for laundromat owners to ask questions), www.wascomat.com/board/index.html

Glossary

Card system: a payment method that involves using prepaid swipe cards (much like phone cards) instead of coins.

Distributor: someone who sells laundry equipment and works for a specific manufacturer in a certain geographic area.

Drop-off: see *wash-and-fold.*

Extractor: a machine that extracts water from laundry by spinning it at a high speed.

Fabricare: the business of taking care of fabric, whether it be wash-and-fold, dry cleaning, or wet cleaning.

Fluff-and-fold: see *wash-and-fold.*

Front-load washer: a large-capacity washing machine that can clean from 18 to 80 pounds of laundry at once; a washer with a door in the front and a drum inside.

Impact fees: also called sewer connection fees or washer hook-up fees; the fees a municipality or water district will charge a laundry business for connecting washers to sewer lines.

Pro forma: an analysis of the expected income and expenses from a laundry business that's for sale.

Pull: collecting coins from machines.

Route operator: someone who services laundry machines in residential buildings such as apartments, condominiums, and dormitories.

Sewer connection fees: see *impact fees.*

Stacked dryer: a piece of equipment that contains two dryers placed one on top of the other in a joined cabinet casing.

Top-load washer: the standard washing machine you find in homes; this type of washer has a door on the top of the machine and an agitator in the middle.

TPD: turns per day; the number of times a machine is used each day.

Tumbler: the horizontal drum inside a dryer or front-load washer.

Turn: one use of a washer.

Wash-and-fold: a service that allows customers to drop off their laundry and have it washed and folded for them; also called drop-off or fluff-and-fold.

Washer hook-up fees: see *impact fees.*

Wet cleaning: an alternative to dry cleaning that uses water rather than solvents to remove dirt and stains from clothing.

Index

U

V

W

Y

Z

Start-Up Guides
Books
Software

To order our catalog call 800-421-2300.
Or visit us online at smallbizbooks.com

Entrepreneur Magazine's
SmallBizBooks.com